WOLFF & BYRD COUNSELORS OF THE MACABRE

CASE FILES, VOL. I

BATTON LASH

SAN DIEGO, CALIFORNIA

This book is dedicated to Mom, Dad, Irene, Billy, Nancy, and Mary.

The stories in this book originally appeared in issues #1 through #4 of *Wolff & Byrd, Counselors of the Macabre.*

Writer/artist: Batton Lash
Editor: Jackie Estrada
Technical consultant: Mitch Berger, Esq.
Art assists: Dennis Caco, Nghia Lam, Derek Ozawa, Melissa Uran
Cover color/separations: In Color
Logo design: Dandy Don Simpson
Staff 'n stuff: S. Derma

Third printing, April 1997

Printed in the United States of America

ISBN #0-9633954-1-6

COME IN! COME IN! DON'T BE AFRAID...
WOLFF & BYRD COUNSELORS OF THE MACABRE

MAY I HELP YOU?
I'M LOOKING FOR LAWYERS, BUT I DIDN'T THINK ANYONE WAS IN HERE . . .
. . . IT'S SO DARK!
OH, THAT'S ONLY BECAUSE WE HAVE A CLIENT HERE WHO'S VERY SENSITIVE TO THE LIGHT . . .

GRRROWLLL

DID YOU HAVE AN APPOINTMENT?
SLAM!

LOOK, I'M HAVING MY FILL OF THE SUPERNATURAL- THAT'S WHAT GOT ME INTO TROUBLE!
HEY, YOU'RE IN THE RIGHT PLACE! MS. WOLFF AND MR. BYRD SPECIALIZE IN CLIENTS WHOSE LEGAL PROBLEMS INVOLVE THE SUPERNATURAL.

RROOARR!

SEE? HE JUST SAID THAT'S WHY HE'S HERE! MY NAME'S MAVIS- I'M WOLFF AND BYRD'S SECRETARY. WHY DON'T YOU COME WITH ME . . .

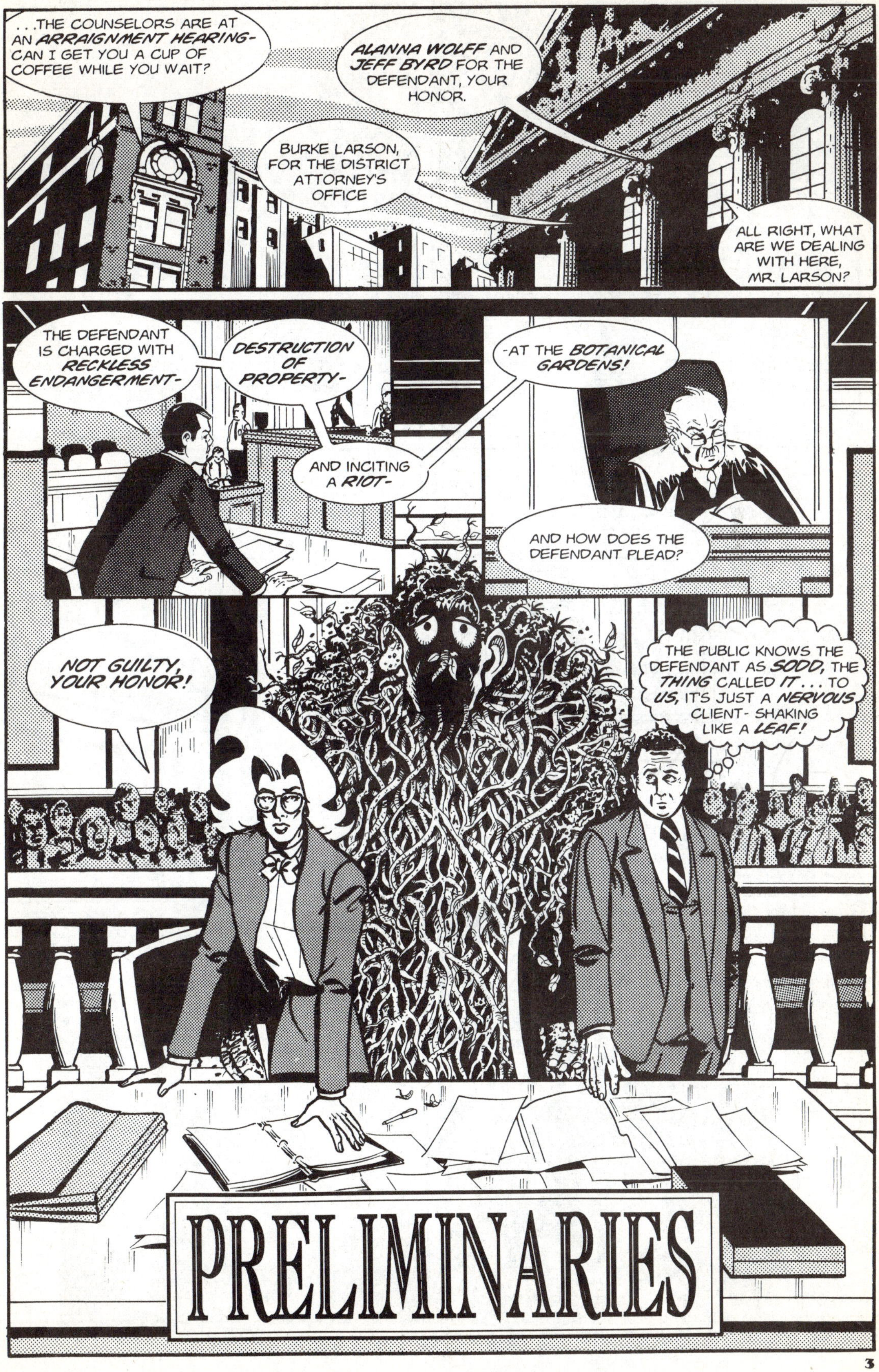

THE DEFENDANT IS CHARGED WITH *RECKLESS ENDANGERMENT*-

DESTRUCTION OF PROPERTY-

AND INCITING A *RIOT*-

-AT THE *BOTANICAL GARDENS!*

AND HOW DOES THE DEFENDANT PLEAD?

NOT GUILTY, YOUR HONOR!

THE PUBLIC KNOWS THE DEFENDANT AS *SODD,* THE *THING* CALLED *IT*... TO *US,* IT'S JUST A *NERVOUS* CLIENT- SHAKING LIKE A *LEAF!*

PRELIMINARIES

YOUR HONOR, WE ASK FOR A *JURY TRIAL*
AND WE ASK THAT THE DEFENDANT BE RELEASED ON HIS OWN *RECOGNIZANCE* PENDING TRIAL

ON WHAT *GROUNDS?*
HE HAS *ROOTS* IN THE COMMUNITY, YOUR HONOR
DOES THE PROSECUTION *OBJECT* TO THE DEFENDANT BEING RELEASED ON HIS OWN RECOGNIZANCE?

YOUR HONOR, AS LONG AS HE STAYS *IN* HIS *ENVIRONMENT*, THE PROSECUTION HAS NO PROBLEM.
I'M SETTING THE STATUS DATE FOR *SIXTY DAYS* FROM NOW. AND A WORD OF *ADVICE* TO MS. WOLFF AND MR. BYRD-

-I HOPE YOU GO OUT ON A *LIMB* FOR YOUR CLIENT- HE'S IN A *HEAP* OF TROUBLE! *NEXT CASE!*
CLOP!

WOLFF, I'M GOING TO CHECK IN WITH *MAVIS* AND SEE WHAT'S GOING ON AT THE *OFFICE*
OK, BYRD. SODD, YOU MIGHT AS WELL GO HOME AND WAIT
ACCORDING TO THE JUDGE, THAT'S *ALL* I CAN DO!
ALANNA-!

I CAN'T *RESIST*- YOUR CLIENT'S *ASS* IS *GRASS*... AND *I'M* THE *LAWNMOWER!* YUK YUK!
YOU PUT THE *CUTE* IN PROSECUTE, LARSON. NOW GET OUT OF MY FACE!

SO THEY'RE THE LAWYERS FOR THE MACK-A-BREE YOU TOLD ME ABOUT?
NOTHING GETS PAST YOU, BOYER- YOU'RE GONNA DO GREAT IN THE D.A.'S OFFICE!

LARSON-- THOSE ATTORNEYS REPRESENT MONSTERS!
DISGUSTING, ISN'T IT?
EVERYBODY HAS A LAWYER THESE DAYS!

BUT TO BE IN SUCH CLOSE PROXIMITY WITH SWAMP CREATURES- VAMPIRES- WEREWOLVES . . .
YEAH, WELL- YOU WANNA TALK ABOUT HORROR-

- I HAVEN'T BEAT 'EM YET IN COURT!
I'M GOING TO USE THE RESTROOM, MS. WOLFF- IT'S THE QUICKEST WAY BACK TO THE SEWER!
OK, WE'LL BE IN TOUCH- JUST DON'T BELIEVE ANYTHING YOU HEAR THROUGH THE GRAPEVINE!

WHAT'S UP AT THE OFFICE, BYRD?
MAVIS WASN'T CARRIED AWAY AGAIN, WAS SHE?
NAH- BUT THE DEMON OF DEKALB AVENUE IS THERE AND WANTS HIS TRANS-CRIPTS. MAVIS SAYS HE'S COMPLAINING THAT WE'RE KEEPING HIM IN THE DARK
HE'S THE ONE SENSITIVE TO LIGHT . . . ANYONE ELSE WAITING FOR US?

SOMEBODY WHO CAME IN COLD- MAVIS SAYS HE'S GOT A CASE THAT COULD USE OUR SERVICES!
LET'S GET BACK THERE, BYRD- IT MAY NOT BE WISE TO HAVE HIM WAIT-ING WITH ONE OF OUR CLIENTS . . .

. . . I CAN'T TELL YOU HOW UPSETTING THIS IS! I'VE NEVER BEEN SUED BEFORE! AND MY WIFE-! CAN'T HANDLE IT. BLAMES EVERY-THING ON ME. DO YOU THINK THAT'S FAIR? I DON'T THINK IT'S FAIR. I GET IT FROM ALL SIDES. FOR INSTANCE . . .
CRIPES! I'VE GOT MY OWN PROBLEMS! WHERE ARE WOLFF AND BYRD? ALL I WANT IS MY TRANSCRIPTS AND TO SLITHER HOME!
AND SO . . .

AFTER THE COUNSELORS RETURN TO THEIR OFFICE AND THEIR CLIENT GETS HIS TRANSCRIPTS . . .
THANKS FOR WAITING, MR. WHITE
HOW CAN WE HELP YOU?
I'M THE VICTIM OF A GHASTLY MISTAKE, MR. BYRD . . .
I WISH I COULD UNDO IT--BUT WISHING IS WHAT GOT ME INTO THIS MESS!!
WHOA! EASY, MR. WHITE . . .
TELL US WHAT HAPPENED . . .
OK, THEN-
HERBERT HAS RISEN FROM THE GRAVE!
I CAN SEE HOW THAT WOULD CAUSE SOME PROBLEMS . . .
WOLFF & BYRD
COUNSELORS OF THE
MACABRE

I'D BETTER TAKE SOME NOTES . . .
LET'S TAKE IT FROM THE TOP, MR. WHITE . . .
WHO'S HERBERT?
HE WAS THE SOB WORLD TO ME AND MY WIFE!
TAKE A LOOK, MS. WOLFF . . . I HAVE A PHOTO RIGHT HERE IN MY WALLET OF HERBERT IN HIS PRIME!

HMM.
WAS HERBERT YOUR SON, MR. WHITE?

HERBERT WAS . . . FAMILY!

THIS IS HERBERT?

YOU BETCHUM- HERBERT WAS ONE IN A MILLION!

AND LOYAL- YOU SHOULD'VE SEEN HOW HE'D WAIT FOR ME TO COME HOME, AND THERE WAS THIS TIME HE WAS HUNGRY-- WELL, LET ME TELL YOU--
AH, MR. WHITE?
YOU WERE TELLING US WHY ACTIONS HAVE BEEN BROUGHT AGAINST YOU . . . ?

(SIGH)--I GUESS IT ALL STARTED THAT DAY I WAS PLAYING WITH HERBERT IN THE PARK...
HEY, PAL, YOU'RE SUPPOSED TO USE A LEASH IN THIS PARK!
WHAT DO YOU HAVE THERE, BOY?

"AT FIRST I THOUGHT HE'D FOUND A BONE- BUT IT WAS SUCH AN ODD-SHAPED THINGIE, I DECIDED TO KEEP IT FOR A BACK SCRATCHER...

"UNFORTUNATELY, MY WIFE WASN'T AS IMPRESSED...
INSTEAD OF TEACHING HERBERT TO BRING JUNK HOME, YOU SHOULD DISCIPLINE HIM!
OLD MAN MORRIS WANTS US TO PAY FOR HIS BEGONIAS THAT HERBERT DUG UP!
YEAH, YEAH,-- SAY, HAVE YOU SEEN MY SLIPPERS?

"I SAT THERE THAT NIGHT, ABSENTLY MINDEDLY SCRATCHING MY BACK...
BOY- I WISH I HAD THE $200 TO GIVE THAT OLD COOT...

IT WAS AT THAT MOMENT, THE BACK SCRATCHER... SCRATCHED!

"THE NEXT DAY WAS HORRIBLE-- I TOOK HERBERT OUT FOR A WALK ... BUT I CAME BACK ALONE!
SO, WHERE'S HERBERT?
HE'S BADLY HURT-- BUT HE'S NOT IN ANY PAIN.
"I TRIED SUBTLETY...

" BUT SHE DIDN'T GET WHAT I WAS TRYING TO SAY! AFTER 20 MINUTES OF HEMMING AND HAWING, I TOLD HER THAT HERBERT HAD BEEN CAUGHT IN THE RUSH HOUR TRAFFIC...
"AND SHE LET OUT A SHRIEK--
YOU DIDN'T HAVE HIM ON A LEASH?!
"MAN, WAS I IN THE DOGHOUSE!

"FOR EVERYTHING!"
BETWEEN THE VET, FOOD, AND REPAIR BILLS, WE SPENT A FORTUNE ON THAT DOG!
AND HERBERT'S LOUSY INSURANCE POLICY ONLY PAID $200--WHICH HAD TO GO TO OLD MAN MORRIS!

"I SPENT MANY NIGHTS ALONE IN FRONT OF THE FIREPLACE . . . I HELD THAT FUNKY BACK SCRATCHER AND IT MADE ME FEEL WISTFUL . . .
OH, I WISH HERBERT WAS HERE . . . SO MY WIFE WOULD LET UP ALREADY!
AND THEN THAT DAMNED THING SCRATCHED ME AGAIN!!
"FEELING THE PRESENCE OF EVIL, I WAS ABOUT TO PITCH IT INTO THE FIRE WHEN I SAW SOMETHING HORRIBLE, SOMETHING SIMIAN STARING BACK AT ME!-
"THAT'S WHEN I HEARD-

SOUND FAMILIAR, BYRD?
YOU BET- THE MONKEY'S PAW!
EH?

IT SOUNDS LIKE HERBERT FOUND THE LEGENDARY TALISMAN!
IT HAD A SPELL PUT ON IT BY AN OLD INDIAN FAKIR, SO IT WOULD BE ABLE TO GRANT THREE WISHES . . .

THE FAKIR WANTED TO SHOW THAT FATE RULES PEOPLE'S LIVES- AND THAT THOSE WHO INTERFERE WITH FATE WILL LIVE TO REGRET IT!

AH.

CAN I CONTINUE?
ER- SURE- BY ALL MEANS . . .

"WHERE WAS I? OH, YEAH- FEELING THE PRESENCE OF EVIL . . . ANYWAY, I WAS ABOUT TO FRY THE BACK SCRATCHER WHEN I HEARD MY WIFE SCREAM-
HE'S BACK!
HE'S BACK!!

HONEY, HAVE YOU GONE *NUTS?!* -- WHAT ARE YOU-
LISTEN, YOU BOOB! IT CAN ONLY BE *HIM!*

SCRITCH SCRITCH SCRITCH

DON'T OPEN THAT DOOR! I WISHED ON THIS THING FOR HERBERT TO COME BACK- BUT I DON'T THINK I *WORDED* IT PROPERLY!
OH, GO SCRATCH YOURSELF!!
HERBERT, BABY! MOMMY'S COMING!

MOMMY'S HERE--

MAYBE IF WE PRETEND WE'RE NOT HOME, IT'LL GO AWAY . . .

"BUT IT DIDN'T! AND WHEN THE NEIGHBORHOOD CAUGHT WIND OF HERBERT, THE FUR BEGAN TO FLY!
. . . AND I'VE BEEN HOUNDED BY LAWSUITS EVER SINCE!
MR. WHITE, WHY DIDN'T YOU USE THE FINAL WISH TO SEND HERBERT BACK TO THE GRAVE?
I WAS GONNA, MS. WOLFF--
YOU ARE HEREBY SUMMONED
SUBPOENA
COMPLAINT:

"BUT I USED A POOR CHOICE OF WORDS . . .
OH, NO! HERE COMES ANOTHER PROCESS SERVER! THEY SEEM TO BE THE ONLY ONES UNFAZED BY *CHOKE* HERBERT!
WE NEED LEGAL HELP! NOW I ONLY WISH I COULD FIND A LAW FIRM THAT COULD HANDLE SOMETHING THIS BIZARRE . . .
SCRATCH SCRATCH SCRATCH

NEXT THING I KNEW, I WAS IN FRONT OF YOUR DOOR!
THEN YOU HAVE THE MONKEY'S PAW WITH YOU?
SURE- WANNA SEE IT? JUST BE CAREFUL WHAT YOU WISH FOR . . .

I DON'T WANT IT FOR WISHING--I WANT TO ENTER IT AS EVIDENCE!
I'LL GET YOU A REPRESENTATIONAL AGREEMENT, MR. WHITE . . . THEN WE CAN GET TO WORK! WE'LL WANT TO SPEAK TO YOUR WIFE . . .
MY WIFE? UH-OH . . .

CAN I USE YOUR PHONE? SHE'S PROBABLY WONDERING WHERE I DISAPPEARED TO . . .
SURE- JUST DIAL "9" FIRST. . .

PART II: ALANNA WOLFF MAKES A MOTION FOR SUMMARY JUDGMENT. WITH HER AT THE BENCH IS MEL GAFFE, THE ATTORNEY FOR THE PLAINTIFFS SUING THE WHITES. THEY STAND BEFORE A JUDGE WHO WILL SOON BE HANDED DOWN A SEVERE RULING ACCORDING TO . . .

THE MONKEY'S LAW!

IT LOOKS LIKE A DECREPIT BACK SCRATCHER TO ME, COUNSELORS!

THAT'S THE MISTAKE OUR CLIENT MADE, YOUR HONOR--IN TRUTH, THIS IS AN ENCHANTED TALISMAN THAT GRANTS WISHES!

THE PAW DELIVERS WHATEVER YOU WISH FOR- BUT BE READY TO SUFFER THE CONSEQUENCES!
HMM- I WISH I WAS ON MY WAY TO FLORIDA! BUT THAT'S NOT GOING TO HAPPEN- NOT WITH MY FULL CALENDAR!

WELL, MS. WOLFF- WE'RE ALL GOING TO SUFFER THE CONSEQUENCES IF WE DON'T GET THIS CASE MOVING!
'SCUSE ME, JUDGE?

SOME FBI AGENTS ARE HERE . . . THEY WANT TO TALK TO YOU ABOUT LAND YOU SOLD IN THE EVERGLADES . . .
WILLIAM W. JACOBS? YOU'VE BEEN INDICTED BY A FLORIDA FEDERAL GRAND JURY. YOU'LL HAVE TO COME WITH US.

YOUR HONOR- WHAT ABOUT THE MOTION FOR SUMMARY JUDGMENT?
I'M TAKING A RECESS OF INDETERMINATE LENGTH--BETTER GET ANOTHER JUDGE TO HEAR THIS CASE!
GASP! THE WISH--IT CAME TRUE!!

ALANNA- THAT WAS JUST A COINCIDENCE, RIGHT? I MEAN, NOTHING'S HAPPENED TO ME--I'M STILL BALD!
MEL, WHAT CAN I TELL YOU? YOU MIGHT'VE LUCKED OUT-
- EVEN THE POWER OF THE MONKEY'S PAW CAN'T CURE BALDNESS!
BEFORE WE GO TO THE TROUBLE OF FINDING A NEW JUDGE, WE SHOULD TRY TO WORK OUT A SETTLEMENT . . .

". . . BUT LET ME TALK TO MY PARTNER FIRST. HE'S WITH OUR CLIENT NOW . . .
. . . AND THERE'S HERBERT. PATHETIC, ISN'T IT, JEFF?
I CAN SEE WHY YOU'D BE UPSET, MR. WHITE . . .

WE ENTER HERBERT IN A DOG SHOW AND MY WIFE DRESSES HIM IN THAT! THE JUDGES PASSED HIM RIGHT BY!
YOU DON'T SEE TOO MANY ROTTWEILERS WEARING BONNETS. BUT SPEAKING OF JUDGES...
MY PARTNER IS IN FRONT OF ONE NOW. IF I CAN GET YOU BOTH TO SIGN THESE AFFIDAVITS...
YOU'RE IN LUCK, JEFF! I FOUND MORE HERBERT PHOTOS!

AHEM YOU SEE, AN AFFIDAVIT IS A SWORN STATEMENT WE CAN SUBMIT TO THE COURT--IT'LL STATE YOU DIDN'T INTENTIONALLY BRING HERBERT BACK FROM THE DEAD.
I DIDN'T WANT HIM TO DIE IN THE FIRST PLACE! IF SOMEONE HAD USED A LEASH LIKE HE WAS SUPPOSED TO-
AGAIN WITH THE LEASH?!

WHY DON'T YOU JUST TAKE ME TO COURT LIKE THE REST OF 'EM?
... BUT A SIGNED AFFIDAVIT MAY BE ALL THE JUDGE REQUIRES TO DISMISS THE CHARGES!
MY WIFE'S SOME-THING, JEFF- WE COULDN'T GO TO THE FUNERAL BECAUSE SHE COULDN'T BEAR TO SEE HIM PUT INTO THE GROUND-

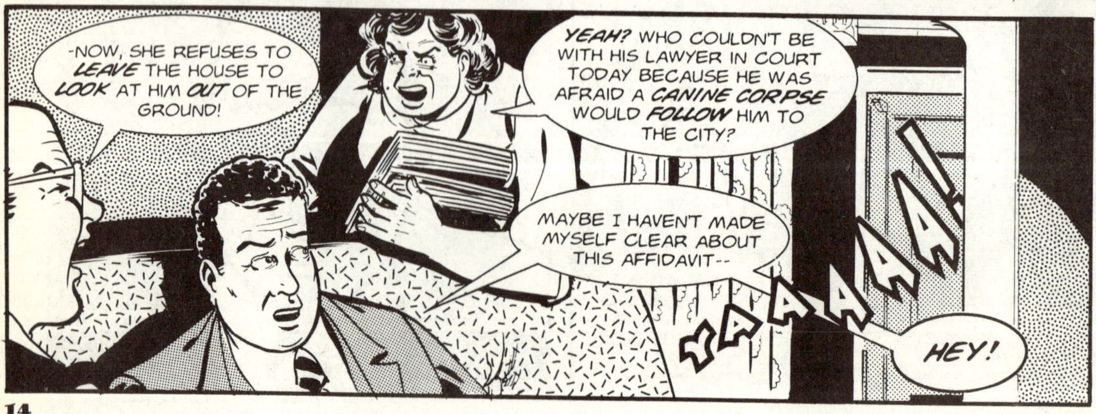
-NOW, SHE REFUSES TO LEAVE THE HOUSE TO LOOK AT HIM OUT OF THE GROUND!
YEAH? WHO COULDN'T BE WITH HIS LAWYER IN COURT TODAY BECAUSE HE WAS AFRAID A CANINE CORPSE WOULD FOLLOW HIM TO THE CITY?
MAYBE I HAVEN'T MADE MYSELF CLEAR ABOUT THIS AFFIDAVIT--
YAAAAA!
HEY!

WHAT THE--? DOGGONE IT!
BEWARE OF DOG

SHEE! FOR A DOG THAT'S DEAD, HE CAN STILL CHASE THE MAILMAN!
THAT DOESN'T MEAN YOU'LL BE RID OF HIM, MRS. WHITE . . .
MAYBE, JUST MAYBE, HERBERT'S NOT COMING BACK THIS TIME!

IS IT THE CURSE, JEFF?
NO, YOUR NEIGHBORS! WHEREVER HERBERT GOES, THEY'RE GOING TO HOLD YOU ACCOUNTABLE FOR HIS BEHAVIOR!
CAN I USE YOUR PHONE? -

"I WANT TO SEE HOW MY PARTNER DID IN COURT TODAY . . .
THAT'S RIGHT, BYRD- JACOBS GOT ARRESTED. OF COURSE I WARNED HIM ABOUT THE MONKEY'S PAW! BUT LIKE MOST PEOPLE, HE HEARD THE WORD "WISH" AND THOUGHT HE WAS DEALING WITH A FAIRY GODMOTHER!
ANYWAY, GAFFE IS OPEN TO A SETTLEMENT. BUT I GOT AN IDEA LOOKING OVER THE PLAINTIFFS' LIST . . .

-ASK THE WHITES' FOR PERMISSION TO EXHUME HERBERT'S GRAVE. YES, I KNOW--TRUST ME ON THIS!
MEL GAFFE'S ON THE LINE- WITH HIS TERMS!
BYRD? GOTTA GO- WHAT'S ALL THAT BARKING IN THE BACKGROUND?

JUST THE WHITES DIS-AGREEING. LISTEN- HERBERT SHAMBLED OFF AFTER THE MAILMAN. . . . YEAH, HE HIGH-TAILED IT.
THERE'S OUR NAME FOR ALL THE WORLD TO SEE, DANGLING OFF A ROTTING ROTTWEILER!
YOU'RE THE ONE WHO INSISTED ON BURYING HIM WITH HIS COLLAR!
YOUR GUESS IS AS GOOD AS MINE, WOLFF- WHO KNOWS WHAT KIND OF PERSPECTIVE A LIVING DEAD DOG HAS ON THE WORLD?

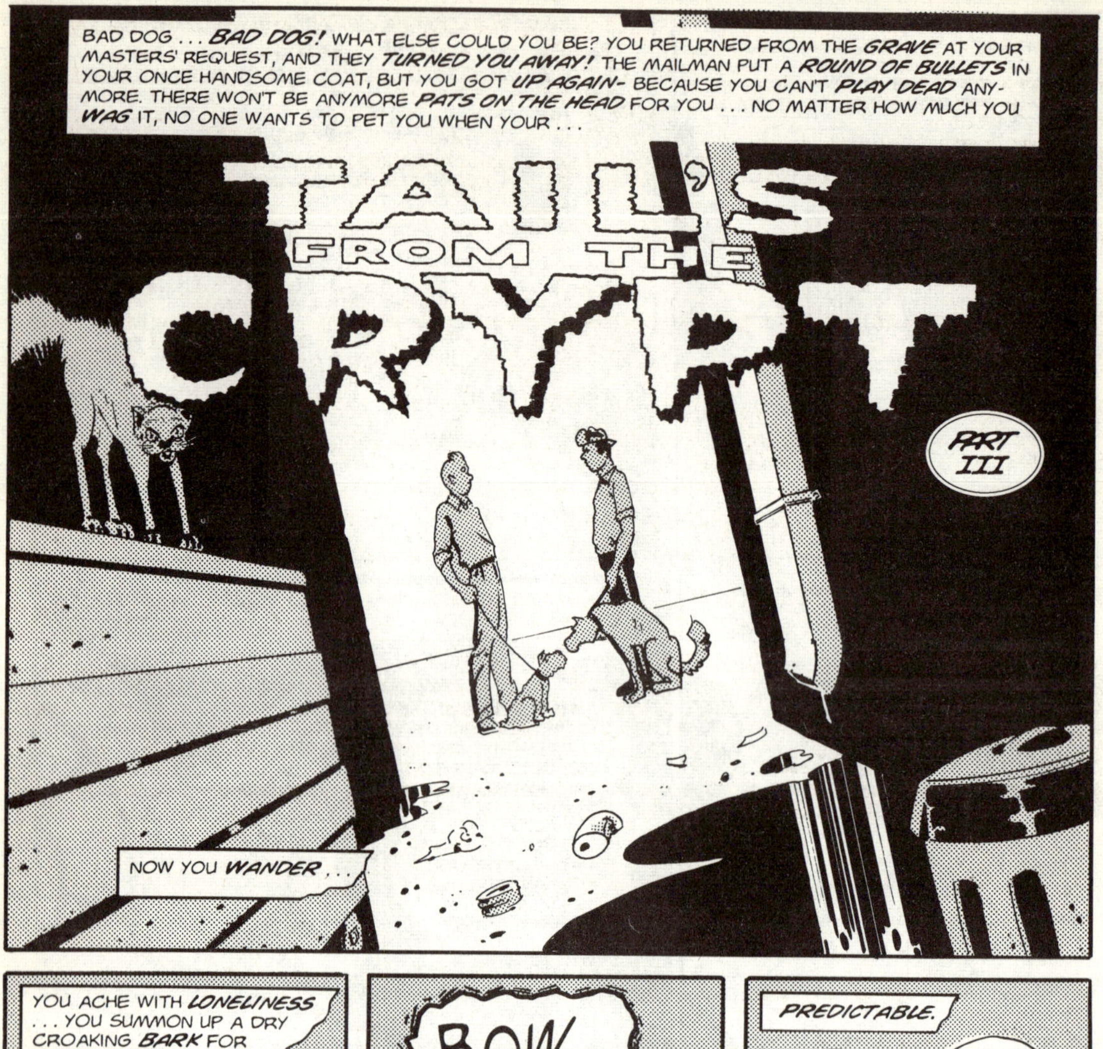

BAD DOG . . . *BAD DOG!* WHAT ELSE COULD YOU BE? YOU RETURNED FROM THE *GRAVE* AT YOUR MASTERS' REQUEST, AND THEY *TURNED YOU AWAY!* THE MAILMAN PUT A *ROUND OF BULLETS* IN YOUR ONCE HANDSOME COAT, BUT YOU GOT *UP AGAIN*- BECAUSE YOU CAN'T *PLAY DEAD* ANYMORE. THERE WON'T BE ANYMORE *PATS ON THE HEAD* FOR YOU . . . NO MATTER HOW MUCH YOU *WAG* IT, NO ONE WANTS TO PET YOU WHEN YOUR . . .

TAIL'S FROM THE CRYPT

PART III

NOW YOU *WANDER* . . .

THEY FLEE FROM THE SIGHT OF YOU. FLEAS FLEE FROM THE SIGHT OF YOU! YOU SHAMBLE ALONG A CURB MARKED WITH MONUMENTS OF HAPPIER TIMES . . . THEN YOU SEE IT- THE PARK!

THE PARK- THE ONLY PLACE WHERE YOU WERE TRULY HAPPY- ROMPING ABOUT, DIGGING HOLES AND PLAYING WITH YOUR MASTER . . .
FETCH, BOY, FETCH!

ON TATTERED HIND LEGS, YOU SIT AND WATCH WITH ENVY . . . YOU GET CLOSER, LICKING YOUR CHOPS, REMEMBERING HOW GOOD IT FELT TO PLAY . . . YOU WANT TO JOIN IN . . .

BUT, YOU FORGOT YOU'RE DEAD- YOU SIT UP AND BEG, BUT IT DOESN'T WIN YOU ANY REWARDS . . .
ROOD RORD!
CHOKE

YOU WERE ONCE MAN'S BEST FRIEND . . . BUT NOW YOU'RE NOT ON SPEAKING TERMS ANYMORE.

IF YELPS COULD COME-- THEY WOULD.
FRISBEE

YOU ARE *SURPRISED* WHEN YOUR LIFELESS NOSTRILS PICK UP A *SCENT* . . .
PHEW! WITH THE *BOOZE* ON THIS GUY'S BREATH, *NO WONDER!*
HIYA, POOCH- I GUESS WE'RE *TWO OF A KIND,* EH?
NOW *INSULT* IS ADDED TO THE *INJURY* . . .

I WASN'T ALWAYS LIKE *THIS,* NO SIR! 'SCUSE ME WHILE I HAVE A LITTLE HAIR OF THE DOG...
GLUG
I WAS ONCE VERY SUCCESSFUL, BUT I WISHED FOR *MORE* . . .
YEAH, I MADE THREE WISHES ON A *CHARM,* AND THEY ALL *BACKFIRED.* I WAS LEFT WITH *NUTHIN'*- EXCEPT FOR THAT DAMN *MONKEY'S PAW!*

I THREW IT AWAY- IT WAS *EVIL!* LAST TIME I SAW IT, A *DOG* WAS CARRYING IT OFF. I HOPE HE BURIED IT *DEEP!*
OH, YOU *POOR, POOR THING!*

THAT IS VERY NICE OF YOU, LADY- BUT I WASN'T ALWAYS LIKE *THIS.* I WAS ONCE VERY-
NOT YOU, YOU BUM! I WAS TALKING TO THAT *PITIFUL CREATURE* . . .

CAN IT BE? YOU OFFER HER YOUR *PAW* . . . WHAT'S *LEFT* OF IT. SHE'S NOT *REVOLTED* . . .
WHO DID *THIS* TO YOU? THEY OUGHT TO BE *SHOT!*
IM GOING TO TAKE YOU HOME AND PUT SOME *FLESH* ON THOSE *BONES!*
YOU THINK THAT'S IN *TERRIBLE TASTE.* YOUR LAST REMAINING SHREDS OF *INSTINCT* TELL YOU THIS DAME IS GOING TO BE *TROUBLE* . . .

HER OVERWHELMING *PERFUME* OFFENDS YOU AND THE *BLUE HAIR* FRIGHTENS YOU . . .
I DON'T LIKE *PEOPLE,* BUT I *WUV WIDDLE DOGGIES!*

GOOD LORD . . . CHOKE . . .
C'MERE . . . *C'MERE* . . .

YOU *BACK OFF.* SOMETHING TELLS YOU *THIS ONE* WOULD MAKE YOU WEAR A *BONNET* ALL THE TIME!
HERE, BOY!
HEERE, BOY . . .

PART IV: HERBERT HAS RISEN FROM THE GRAVE- OR HAS HE JUST RETURNED FROM THE DEAD? THAT'S THE QUESTION *WOLFF AND BYRD* ASK. WITH THEIR CLIENTS' PERMISSION, THE COUNSELORS GET A COURT ORDER TO EXHUME HERBERT'S GRAVE, SO THEY CAN COME TO . . .

TERMS OF INTERMENT

LOOKING AT THE PLAINTIFF LIST, I NOTICED THAT *EVERYONE* WAS JUMPING ON THE GRAVY TRAIN TO SUE THE WHITES- *EXCEPT* THE PET CEMETERY!

SPAID SHOULD'VE BEEN THE *FIRST* ONE TO CALL THE POLICE ABOUT A GRAVE ROBBING- BUT HOW COULD HE, SINCE HERBERT WAS *NEVER* BURIED HERE!

I GOT MEL GAFFE TO AGREE THAT ANY *RESTITUTION* MONEY THE WHITES GET FROM SPAID WILL GO TO THE PLAINTIFFS HE REPRESENTS ...

THEN ALL THAT REMAINS IS *HERBERT'S* REMAINS- LET'S GET THE WHITES TO SIGN THAT AGREEMENT NOW!

REX R.I.P.

SHORTLY ...

I'M OUTTA HERE, MR. BYRD! SEE YOU TOMORROW!

REMEMBER, MAVIS- THERE'LL BE A *FULL MOON*- YOU'LL BE WORKING *LATE!*

DO YOU HAVE ANY QUESTIONS ABOUT THE SETTLEMENT, MR. WHITE?

I READ THIS AGREEMENT UNTIL IT WAS DOG-EARED ... AND I STILL CAN'T *UNDERSTAND* THE *LEGALESE!*

YOU'VE GONE OVER IT ENOUGH TIMES WITH US FOR *ME* TO UNDERSTAND. *ONE* THING, THOUGH ...

RIGHT HERE WHERE IT SAYS HERBERT WILL BE RETURNED TO THE GRAVE BY USING THE MONKEY'S PAW VIA A *DESIGNATED WISHOR* ...

WHAT ABOUT IT, MRS. WHITE?

I'D LIKE TO BE THE ONE WHO MAKES THAT WISH! IT--IT WOULD MEAN A LOT TO ME.
NO PROBLEM WITH ME- OF COURSE, WE'VE GOT TO GET THE OKAY FROM THE PLAINTIFFS' COUNSEL . . .
HOW ABOUT IT, MEL?

FINE WITH ME--BUT LET'S GET ON WITH IT! I'M LATE FOR AN APPOINTMENT WITH MY ELECTROLYSIST!
MR. AND MRS. WHITE, ONCE YOU'VE SIGNED THE AGREEMENT, WE CAN COMMENCE WITH THE READING OF THE WISH . . .
WE'RE OVER HERE, MEL!

AND AFTER THE FORMALITIES HAVE BEEN COMPLETED . . .
ANYTIME YOU'RE READY, MRS. WHITE. HOLD THE PAW WHILE YOU READ FROM THE AGREEMENT . . .
I'M READY . . .
"I DO HEREBY WISH-

"-INFER, COMMAND, DIRECT, AND PROPOUND THAT HERBERT SHALL AND WITH DELIBERATE SPEED RETURN TO-
GLUB

MRS. WHITE?
SNIF LET ME TRY AGAIN . . .

"I DO HEREBY WISH, INFER, COMMAND, DIRECT, AND PROPOUND THAT HERBERT SHALL AND WITH DELIBERATE SPEED RETURN TO-

-HIS LOVING MASTERS!!
THAT'S NOT WHAT WE AGREED ON!!
OH BOY
NO KIDDING, MEL

MEL, COULD WE HAVE A FEW MINUTES ALONE WITH OUR CLIENTS?
HERBERT!
SCRITCH SCRITCH SCRITCH
GROAN IT'S BAD ENOUGH I HAVE ALL THIS HAIR, NOW YOU'RE GOING TO TURN IT GRAY!

COUNSELORS, LET ME TALK TO HER--SHIRLEY, I THOUGHT YOU WERE REPULSED BY HERBERT!
THE WAY HE IS NOW, I AM! BUT I REMEMBER THE LIVE HERBERT- AND THAT THING OUT THERE IS STILL HERBERT-

—THAT'S WHY I FEEL SO GUILTY ABOUT SENDING HIM TO A COLD, LONELY GRAVE! YOU'RE LAWYERS-- WORD THE AGREEMENT IN A WAY THAT WILL BRING THE REAL HERBERT BACK!
SORRY, MRS. WHITE
NO CAN DO!

EVEN THE MOST CAREFULLY WORDED WISH GUIDED BY THE BEST OF INTENTIONS WILL BE TWISTED AND BRING NOTHING BUT MISERY...
YOU CAN'T WIN WITH THE MONKEY'S PAW!

SHIRL- IF YOU DON'T DO IT, SOMEONE ELSE WILL. MAKE THE WISH- LET HERBERT REST IN PEACE.
THE POOR THING- LISTEN TO HIM!
SCRITCH
SCRITCH
SCRITCH

:SIGH: I WISH I HAD THE COURAGE TO SEND HIM OFF TO HIS FINAL REWARD...

WHAT ARE WE WAITING FOR? THAT MANGY ODOR IS MAKING ME SICK!
BUT YOU SAID-
YEAH, WELL, WHEN YOU GOTTA GO, YOU GOTTA GO! "I DO HEREBY WISH, INFER, COMMAND, AND PROPOUND ..."
MEL, COME BACK IN!

A FEW WEEKS LATER-
WELL, WOLFF, WE GOT THE SETTLEMENT FROM SPAID- BUT I CAN'T BELIEVE THE D.A. WON'T PRESS CHARGES AGAINST HIM FOR FRAUD!
SHE PROBABLY THOUGHT IT WAS JUST ANOTHER SHAGGY DOG STORY FROM US, BYRD-

-ESPECIALLY WHEN YOU MENTIONED THE MONKEY'S PAW!
I THOUGHT IT WAS RELEVANT
IT'S BEEN A MOOT POINT EVER SINCE YOU WISHED FOR A PLACE TO KEEP THE PAW SAFE--WE HAVEN'T SEEN IT SINCE!
OK, SO I WAS SCRATCHING MY BACK WHEN I SAID IT- SLIP OF THE TONGUE!

AS FOR SPAID- CALL IT WISHFUL THINKING ON MY PART, BUT I THINK WE'LL SEE HIM IN FRONT OF A JUDGE BEFORE LONG . . .
REALLY?
YOU KNOW WHAT THEY SAY, BYRD . . .

"EVERY DOG HAS ITS DAY . . . IN COURT!
AARGH!! NOT AGAIN!

YOU ONCE LONGED FOR YOUR LIFE AS HERBERT . . . BUT NOW, IN DEATH, YOU'VE NEVER BEEN HAPPIER!
FIRST THOSE LAWYERS, NOW THIS! IF ANYONE SEES ALL THESE EMPTY GRAVES . . . !

IT'S AS IF SOMEONE WISHED YOU'D BE AT PEACE IN THE CEMETERY--AND YOU ARE!
OUT, DAMNED SPOT!!

YOU'RE IN YOUR NEW PARK-- ROMPING ABOUT, DIGGING HOLES, AND YOUR NEW MASTER EVEN WANTS TO PLAY FETCH . . .
EEYAHHH!
LET'S FACE IT- YOU'RE A LUCKY DOG!
END

"IT WAS OUR *DREAM HOUSE--* GREAT LOCATION, QUIET STREET, ONLY 5% INTEREST, AND NO *FEES!*

"IT EVEN HAD *TWO* BATHROOMS . . . BUT ONCE A *MONTH* OUR JOY TURNED TO *FEAR* . . .

"AND IT WASN'T BECAUSE OF THE MORTGAGE PAYMENT! NO, COUNSELOR, IT WAS THE *FULL MOON!*

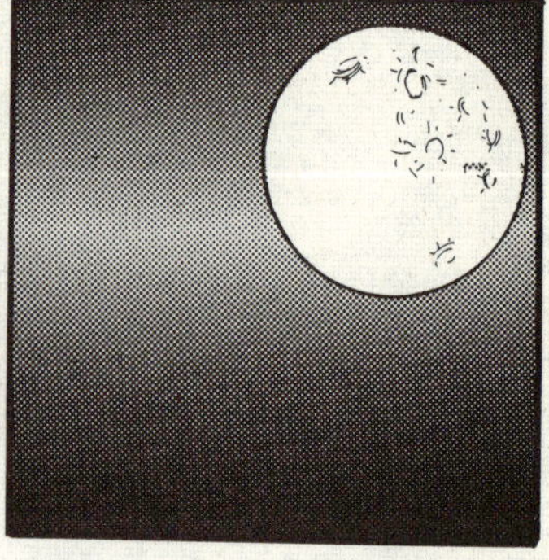

"AT FIRST I THOUGHT WE WERE HAVING NIGHTMARES! BUT THEN TOM'S *BOSS* CAME FOR DINNER. . .

" . . . AND WE REALIZED THAT SOMETHING WAS WRONG-- *HORRIBLY WRONG!*

"THAT'S WHEN I MADE THE CONNECTION WITH THE FULL MOON . . . IT WAS THE *ONLY* ANSWER!

" ⸗CHOKE⸗ YES, OUR SWEET LITTLE HOUSE GOES THROUGH AN *UNHOLY TRANSFORMATION* EVERY 28 DAYS WHEN IT SUFFERS FROM THE . . .

CURSE OF THE WERE-HOUSE!

I'LL SUE!! Y'HEAR? I'LL SUE YOU FOR EVERYTHING YOU OWN!

THAT'S MY WIFE'S THEORY! I SAY THERE'S A LOGICAL EXPLANATION FOR WHAT'S HAPPENING TO OUR HOME!
DID I MENTION THAT MY HUSBAND'S IN MAJOR DENIAL?
WELL, MRS. CURTIS- I'D HAVE TO AGREE WITH YOUR HUSBAND . . .

. . . YOUR EYES CAN PLAY TRICKS ON YOU AT NIGHT, THE WEATHER CAN CAUSE A HOUSE TO MAKE ODD NOISES, AND SO FORTH . . .
WHY, IF I WENT TO COURT AND SAID YOUR HOUSE WAS HAUNTED- I'D BE RIDICULED FOR THAT KIND OF DEFENSE!
LOOK, MR. MEYER- I DON'T BELIEVE IN GHOSTS--

-BUT I DO BELIEVE MY EX-BOSS WILL PURSUE HIS PERSONAL INJURY SUIT AGAINST US!
AND I TELL YOU, SOMETHING WEIRD HAPPENS TO OUR HOME EVERY FULL MOON!
EH-EH- TELL YOU WHAT . . .

. . . LET ME SPEND THE NIGHT AT YOUR HOUSE. EH-EH . . . I'LL FIND PLAUSIBLE EXPLANATIONS FOR ALL YOUR SPOOKS . . .
I'M A NATURAL DEBUNKER, I'M AFRAID . . .

AND ON THE NEXT FULL MOON . . .
YAARGH!

MR. MEYER!!
GASP! HE WAS SO FRIGHTENED, HIS HAIR TURNED WHITE!
AYYAAAH!

THIS . . . THIS IS TERRIBLE! I SEE ANOTHER LAWSUIT COMING!!
TOM- NOW CAN WE CALL IN SPECIALISTS?
EH . . .
EH . . .
EH . . .

WOLFF & BYRD
COUNSELORS OF THE
MACABRE
OH, NO- THEM! I TOLD YOU WE SHOULD'VE GONE STRAIGHT BACK TO THE DA'S OFFICE AFTER THE HEARING!
QUIET, BOYER- I CAN HANDLE HER . . .
GO GET HIM, WOLFF. I'LL STAY WITH THE CLIENT . . .
LARSON! YOU AND I HAVE TO TALK ABOUT WHAT WENT ON IN THAT STATUS HEARING!
FOR GOD'S SAKE, LARSON--DON'T GET HER ANGRY!
I'M NOT HAPPY, LARSON . . .
HEY! THE JUDGE RULED! WE HAVE NOTHING TO TALK ABOUT!
SHE'S GOING TO GET ONE OF HER CLIENTS TO TURN US INTO TOADS! AND SHE'LL MAKE SURE IT'S ALL LEGAL!!
UNLESS, OF COURSE, YOU WANT TO DISCUSS YOUR CLIENT TAKING THE PLEA OFFER . . .?
YOU'RE BARKING UP THE WRONG TREE, LARSON-

I WANT TO TALK TO YOU ABOUT THE EVIDENCE THE POLICE PRUNED FROM MY CLIENT . . .
. . . WE'RE GOING TO FILE A MOTION TO SUPPRESS!
GO AHEAD--

YOU DO AND THERE'LL BE NO PLEA OFFER!
MAYBE I SHOULD TAKE THE PLEA, MR. BYRD . . .
NO WAY! THE CASE I'M LOOKING AT SHOWS THAT WHAT THE POLICE DID TO YOU WAS WRONG!

LOOK, IT'S GOING TO COME OUT THAT THE PROSECUTION HAS TAINTED EVIDENCE, AND YOU'RE GOING TO HAVE TO FACE THE CONSEQUENCES!
TELL IT TO THE JUDGE, ALANNA-

NOT ONLY DO YOU HAVE TO CONVINCE HIM THAT I MADE A MISTAKE- BUT YOU HAVE TO CONVINCE HIM THAT HE MADE ONE, TOO! BRR!
IF THE JUDGE DOESN'T LISTEN, THE COURT OF APPEALS WILL!

SURE! BUT IN THE MEANTIME YOUR CLIENT'LL BE DOING TIME AT THE STATE PRISON FARM- WHERE HE BELONGS!
BOYER! WHY'D YOU FORGET MY UMBRELLA?
I TELL YOU, LARSON- WOLFF 'N BYRD ARE BEHIND THIS DOWN-POUR! THAT'S ONE LAW FIRM THAT PROBABLY HAS A REAL RAINMAKER!
UH OH, IT'S STARTING TO RAIN AGAIN, MR. BYRD . . .
HOPE YOU DON'T MIND, SODD-

-BUT I'D RATHER NOT STAND UNDER YOU DURING A STORM!
WHY WERE YOU TALKING TO THE ASSISTANT D.A., MS. WOLFF?
I HAD TO LET LARSON KNOW THAT HE MAY HAVE FOOLED THE JUDGE, BUT HE DIDN'T FOOL ME!
HE MAY SAY THAT THE POLICE WERE PRUNING FOR EVIDENCE- -BUT IN YOUR CASE IT'S CALLED AMPUTATION!
WE'RE HEADING BACK TO THE OFFICE, SODD. WE'LL BE IN TOUCH . . . MAKE SURE NOBODY BUILDS A TREEHOUSE IN YOU - THEY MIGHT HOLD YOU LIABLE IF ANYTHING HAPPENS TO THEM!

SHORTLY-
OF ALL THE ROTTEN LUCK- SODD GOT CAUGHT IN THE DOWNPOUR ON THE WAY TO COURT! WITH SODD IN FULL BLOOM, THE JUDGE BLAMED HIM FOR HIS ALLERGY ATTACK!
YEAH, WELL- IT DIDN'T HELP THAT THE JUDGE HAD WATCHED "THE DAY OF THE TRIFFIDS" LAST NIGHT . . .
MAVIS . . . ?

HI YA, COUNSELORS! YOUR SECRETARY LOOKED LIKE SHE COULD USE A MASSAGE . . . AFTER SITTING AT THIS DESK ALL DAY . . .
MANOMAN . . . THIS GUY KNOWS HOW TO GIVE A BACK RUB!

WELL, I'D LIKE TO TAKE YOU UP ON ONE OF THOSE BACK RUBS- AFTER WE GO OVER YOUR CASE . . .
I'M INNOCENT! I HAD NOTHING TO DO WITH THAT ARMED ROBBERY . . .
I'LL BE IN AS SOON AS I CHECK MY MESSAGES, WOLFF . . .
OOOH YES . . . BEST MASSAGE I EVER HAD- HANDS DOWN!

MR. BYRD! YOU LOOK LIKE YOU'VE JUST SEEN A GHOST!
A GHOST I CAN DEAL WITH, MAVIS! SOMETHING THAT'S HAUNTED ME FOR YEARS IS ANOTHER MATTER . . .

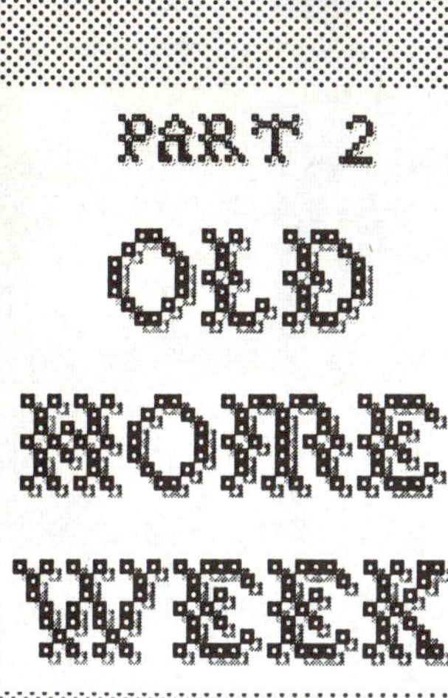
PART 2
OLD HOME WEEK

IMAGINE MY SURPRISE HEARING FROM YOU AFTER ALL THESE YEARS, KIM-- AND THIS BUSINESS ABOUT YOUR HOUSE!
HAVE YOU HAD PARANORMAL PSYCHOLOGISTS INVESTIGATE IT?
UH-HUH. BUT I HAD TO DO IT WITHOUT TOM KNOWING.
THE SUPERNATURAL IS NOT A SUBJECT HE TOLERATES.

TOM- YOUR HUSBAND?
YES . . . HE THREW A FIT WHEN HE CAME HOME ONE DAY TO FIND PSYCHIC RESEARCHERS TAPPING THE WALLS!

WE HAD A BIG FIGHT OVER THAT. TO MAKE MATTERS WORSE, THE INVESTIGATORS COULD FIND NO TRACE OF SUPERNATURAL PHENOMENA.
BUT AFTER THE LAST INCIDENT-

I REALIZED THAT THE HOUSE ONLY CHANGES UNDER A FULL MOON!
THIS LAST INCIDENT INVOLVED TOM'S BOSS?

YES.. IT WAS THE FIRST TIME SOMEONE OTHER THAN ME AND TOM EXPERIENCED OUR HOME'S TRANSFORMATION. TOM WAS SCARED OUT OF HIS WITS-

-WHEN HE WAS FIRED AND SLAPPED WITH A WHOPPING PERSONAL INJURY SUIT! OUR ATTORNEY WAS A TAD INTIMIDATED BY THE CASE, SO TOM GAVE IN AND LET ME CALL YOU.
GAVE IN?

I'VE BEEN READING ABOUT YOUR FIRM IN THE PAPERS FOR YEARS. TOM DISMISSED IT AS TABLOID TRASH. I TOLD HIM I KNEW YOU WHEN--BACK WHEN WE WERE IN THE TRENCHES AT CHASE HAWKINS' FIRM

OH- AND THAT CONVINCED HIM?
NOT REALLY- HE TOLD ME TO CALL CHASE HAWKINS.

HA HA HA HA HA
AND? DID YOU CALL OUR OLD BOSS?

I TOLD TOM I WORKED FOR CHASE IN A STOREFRONT LAW FIRM WAY BEFORE HE BECAME A BIGSHOT PARK AVENUE ATTORNEY. WE'D NEVER AFFORD HIM NOW.
SO THAT LED TO ANOTHER FIGHT. I HAD TO ARGUE THAT YOUR FIRM WAS WHAT WE NEEDED.
SOUNDS LIKE A GUY USED TO HAVING HIS WAY.

JEFF, IT'S BEEN DIFFICULT. WE ALMOST SPLIT UP A YEAR AGO. HE DIDN'T WANT A CHILD--I DID. AFTER COUNSELING, WE DECIDED TO STAY TOGETHER . . . I THOUGHT IF WE BOUGHT A HOUSE, HE'D RECONSIDER RAISING A FAMILY-
BUT NOW WHAT WE HAVE IS AN EXTENDED FAMILY THAT RISES ONCE A MONTH TO HAUNT OUR HOME!
KIM . . .

I'LL TALK TO MY PARTNER AND SEE WHAT WE CAN DO. THERE'S A FULL MOON IN A COUPLE OF DAYS. MAYBE WE'LL COME BY AND CHECK IT OUR FOR OURSELVES. HOW'S THAT SOUND?
GREAT. BY THE WAY . . .

YOUR PARTNER . . . ARE YOU AND SHE . . . ?
STRICTLY A PROFESSIONAL RELATIONSHIP. I'M SINGLE, SHE'S SINGLE, AND NEVER THE TWAIN SHALL MEET.

YOU'RE SWEET, JEFF. AND THEY SAY NICE GUYS AREN'T AVAILABLE ANYMORE . . .

I WAS SO SELF-CONSCIOUS BACK THEN-REALLY OVERWEIGHT . . . I WAS INTIMIDATED BY CHASE HAWKINS' CONSTANTLY FLIRTING WITH KIM! IT WAS PRACTICALLY HARASSMENT! NO WONDER SHE QUIT. SHE WANTED TO MOVE ON- AND I WASN'T PART OF HER FUTURE!

YOU'VE COME A LONG WAY SINCE I FIRST MET YOU, MR. BYRD. BUT I HAVE TO ASK- HOW MUCH EXCESS BAGGAGE ARE YOU BRINGING WITH YOU ON THIS CASE?

THE HOUSE BOO FULL
THIS MUST BE THE PLACE, WOLFF . . . !
IF IT ISN'T, THIS HOUSE HAS THE WORST CASE OF DRY ROT IVE EVER SEEN . . .
JEFF!
YOU MUST BE ALANNA WOLFF- THE HOUSE IS A MESS, BUT COME ON IN . . .
I MUST WARN YOU-- MY HUSBAND'S SKEPTICAL ABOUT HIRING YOUR FIRM, BUT FEELS HE HAS NO CHOICE-
HE'S AT THE END OF HIS- OH!
PART 3

IS- IS THAT TOM?
I'M JUST A HOME BODY, HANGING AROUND!
I DON'T KNOW WHO THAT IS-- BUT HE STARTLES ME EVERY TIME!
CYPRESS!

CRRREEEAAKKK
KIM...
WHERE ARE YOU, KIM...
I'VE BEEN LOOKING FOR YOU...

THERE YOU ARE! I WAS GETTING DRESSED WHEN THE WALL OPENED AND I GOT LOST IN A SECRET CORRIDOR... ARE THESE THE LAWYERS?
TOM! THE HANGING MAN! HE'S BACK! LOOK--!

WHERE? IT'S JUST SHADOWS FROM A TREE!
OKAY- SO EXPLAIN WHERE THE SECRET CORRIDOR CAME FROM, WISE GUY!
BYRD- WEVE GOT OUR WORK CUT OUT FOR US WITH THIS GUY!

AND SO...
I'D OFFER YOU A CHAIR, BUT IT MAY RUN OFF WITH YOU. LET'S GET ON WITH IT. WHAT'S THE STORY WITH MY EX-BOSS?
IT'S A MATTER OF PROVING THAT SUPERNATURAL FORCES YOU HAD NO CONTROL OVER WERE RESPONSIBLE FOR THE PLAINTIFF'S INJURIES AND NOT YOU.
ONCE WE DO THAT, IT'S LIKELY HE'LL DROP THE SUIT AND YOUR HOMEOWNER'S INSURANCE SHOULD COVER HIS MEDICAL EXPENSES.
"SUPERNATURAL FORCES," EH? HOW MUCH AM I PAYING YOU GUYS AN HOUR?
OH, C'MON, TOM- ALANNA- WHO'S 'CYPRESS'?

JACK CYPRESS BUILT THIS HOUSE 75 YEARS AGO. HE WAS A DEVOTED FOLLOWER OF OCCULTIST ABNER WARWICK AND LONGED TO BE HIS SUCCESSOR IN MASTERING THE BLACK ARTS!
UNFORTUNATELY FOR CYPRESS, HE NEVER RECEIVED THE NOTORIETY HE DESIRED-WE FOUND COURT RECORDS FROM 1932 WHEN TREASURY AGENTS HAD ARRESTED HIM, MISTAKING HIS ARCANE POTIONS FOR ILLEGAL MOONSHINE!
AT HIS HEARING, HE EXPLAINED THAT HIS HOUSE WAS BUILT FROM WOOD TAKEN FROM A FOREST WHERE WOLFBANE GREW--A VARIETY KNOWN AS TIMBER WOLF. CYPRESS INVITED THE PRESS TO COME OVER AND WATCH HIS HOME TRANSFORM ON THE NEXT FULL MOON. UNFORTUNATELY FOR HIM, NOTHING HAPPENED . . . BUT BAD PRESS!
HOUSE NOT HAUNTED BUT OWNER HAS BATS IN BELFRY
ACCORDING TO CYPRESS'S OBITUARY, HE BECAME DESTITUTE AFTER THE PRESS FIASCO . . . THE GOVERNMENT SEIZED HIS HOUSE FOR NONPAYMENT OF TAXES. HE HUNG HIMSELF, LEAVING BEHIND A SUICIDE NOTE:
I'll be back– and on page one, too! Jack Cypress
WE CAN ONLY GUESS THAT WHEN CYPRESS PAINTED HIS HOME, HE USED A LEAD-BASED PAINT THAT SHIELDED THE WERE-LUMBER FROM THE MOONLIGHT . . .
HUNG HIMSELF?
HUH! FEDERAL REGULATIONS FORBADE US TO MOVE IN UNTIL WE'D REMOVED EVERY BIT OF LEAD PAINT . . .
OOOKAY . . . I'M GOING TO MAKE SOME COFFEE BEFORE THE CUPS GO FLYING . . .

THIS IS ABNER WARWICK- 19TH CENTURY OCCULTIST WHOM CYPRESS IDOLIZED!
HMPH! THE OTHER 28 DAYS OF THE MONTH, THAT PAINTING'S AN ORIGINAL HOCKNEY!

SO WHAT ARE YOU TELLING ME? SOME WANNABE HEXED MY HOUSE? ARE YOU FOR REAL?
THE SUPERNATURAL EXISTS, MR. CURTIS- WHETHER YOU BELIEVE IN IT OR NOT!

THE MOST FRIGHTENING ASPECT OF THE SUPERNATURAL IS HOW IT CAN AFFECT PEOPLE ON A LEGAL LEVEL.
BY STAYING IN THE DARK ABOUT DARK FORCES, ONE RUNS THE RISK OF THE COURTS TAKING A-
DON'T PATRONIZE ME, DUDE-

HEY, I'M NOT--
IT'S BAD ENOUGH I'VE HIRED LAWYERS WHO CHASE HEARSES INSTEAD OF AMBULANCES!
HOLD ON, MR. CURTIS-

YOU'VE NEVER BEEN IN A LEGAL SITUATION LIKE THIS-
ALL I KNOW IS-EH?
CRASH!
KIM!

I'LL BE ALL RIGHT. I WAS FIXING THE COFFEE AND SAW SOMEONE STARING AT ME- I MUST HAVE FAINTED.
WAS IT A GHOST?

NO- JUST A NOSY NEIGHBOR! EVER SINCE THE TRANSFORMATIONS STARTED, THE GUY NEXT DOOR KEEPS PEEKING IN TO SEE WHAT'S GOING ON! I GUESS IT'S UNDERSTANDABLE . . .
KIM, EVEN THOUGH YOU LIVE IN A HAUNTED HOUSE, YOU'RE STILL ENTITLED TO YOUR PRIVACY . . .

. . . I CAN GET A RESTRAINING ORDER AGAINST A PEEPING TOM SO FAST IT WOULD MAKE HIS HEAD SPIN!
COUNSELORS, WHY DON'T WE CALL IT A NIGHT . . .

. . . IT'S BEEN A LITTLE STRESSFUL FOR US . . . AND I'M SAYING THINGS I KNOW I'LL REGRET. LET ME CALL YOUR OFFICE TOMORROW.
I UNDERSTAND, MR. CURTIS.
THANKS FOR COMING BY . . . I DON'T KNOW WHAT CAME OVER ME!
TAKE CARE, KIM.

I DON'T KNOW WHAT CAME OVER HER, EITHER-- WHAT WAS SHE THINKING WHEN SHE MARRIED THAT BUTTHEAD?
HMM- WHOSE DEMONS ARE COMING OUT NOW, "DUDE"?

DON'T REMIND ME! IF THE SUPERNATURAL IS TOO FAR-FETCHED FOR TOM, HE'S ABOUT TO GET HIS SHARE OF REALITY-- IN SPADES...

. . . KIM'S ASKED ME TO RECOMMEND A DIVORCE ATTORNEY FOR HER!
GET AWAY FROM THE WINDOW!

SHUSH! NOW WHO ARE THOSE TWO?
LAWYERS! DON'T YOU SEE WHAT'S GOING ON OVER THERE, CHARLOTTE?

THE SCREAMS AND THE MOANS THROUGH THE NIGHT . . .
. . . THE THUMPING AND BANGING . . .
WEIRD FIGURES IN TATTERED CLOTHES WANDERING AIMLESSLY . . .
. . . THAT HORRIBLE MUSIC . . .
STRANGE ODORS- THE EERIE, GLOWING LIGHT . . .

JEEZ LOUISE! I'VE HEARD STORIES . . . I'VE BEEN AROUND . . . I KNOW WHAT HAPPENED TO THAT HOUSE!!
THE CURTISES SEEMED LIKE SUCH A NICE COUPLE . . . BUT THOSE ARE THE ONES YOU HAVE TO WATCH OUT FOR!

WELL, I'M NOT GOING TO STAND FOR IT!
GASP! WHO ARE YOU GONNA CALL-- ??

PART 4 UNREAL ESTATE

WE HAVE REASON TO BELIEVE THE BUREAU OF FIREARMS AND DRUGS IS PLANNING A RAID ON OUR CLIENTS-
B.F.D.

-THEIR HOME MAY BE POSSESSED, BUT NOT OF CONTROLLED SUBSTANCES!
THE DEPT. OF JUSTICE DOES NOT CONFIRM OR DENY THAT, MS. . . .
MS. WOLFF, IS IT?

THAT'S RIGHT- AND I HOPE YOU REMEMBER MY NAME- BECAUSE I'LL BE DEPOSING YOU IF MY CLIENTS' RIGHTS ARE VIOLATED.
THE BFD CAN COME IN AND LOOK AROUND THE CURTISES' HOME AND SEE FOR THEMSELVES THAT THERE ARE NO DRUGS- DEMONS, MAYBE, BUT NO DRUGS!
LIKE I SAID, MISTER --- ?

BYRD.
BYRD, YES . . . I'M NOT AT LIBERTY TO SAY IF THIS IS AN INVESTIGATION. THAT IS NOT TO SAY THERE IS ONE . . .

BUT IF THERE WERE AN INVESTIGATION-
AND I'M NOT SAYING THERE IS--
-THE BFD WOULDN'T WANT YOUR CLIENTS TO HAVE ADVANCE WARNING TO CLEAN HOUSE, NOW, WOULD WE?

NOBODY MOVE!

CLEAR!
MOVE IN!
SEARCH EVERY INCH OF THE HOUSE!
MOVE IT!!

KNOCK DOWN THIS WALL- THERE MAY BE STUFF HIDDEN BEHIND IT!
IN HERE! I FOUND THE OWNERS!
BFD

JEEZ LOUISE!
OKAY, YOU TWO-

- PUT YOUR HANDS UP AND OVER YOUR HEADS!
NOW WAIT JUST A MINUTE!
DO AS HE SAYS, CHARLOTTE!
FIND ANYTHING?
NOTHING YET, SIR.
LOOK IN THE BASEMENT.
WEVE TORN DOWN THE BEDROOM WALL- NOTHING!
RIP UP THE FLOOR AND KEEP LOOKING!
I'D SAY WEVE GOT A GOOD HALF HOUR TO GO-

- BEFORE THE BFD ADMITS THEY HAVE THE WRONG ADDRESS!
HOW COULD THE GOVERNMENT THINK I'M RUNNING A DRUG RACKET OUT OF MY HOME?
I ALWAYS SAID NO TO DRUGS! DRUG TESTING WAS A REQUIREMENT FOR MY JOB- DOESN'T THE BFD CHECK ON THAT?
THE BFD ACTS NOW AND THINKS LATER, MR. CURTIS

THIS ISN'T A CRACK HOUSE, IT'S A HAUNTED HOUSE! DOESN'T THE BFD REALIZE THERE ARE FORCES BEYOND THEIR MORTAL KEN THAT HAVE NOTHING TO DO WITH DRUGS? HOW CLOSED MINDED CAN THEY BE?
TOM- GET A GRIP!
THE BFD IS HERE, AND WE HAVE TO DEAL WITH THEM-

-GOOD THING WE GOT HERE BEFORE THE HOUSE TRANSFORMED. IF THE BFD SEES WHAT REALLY GOES ON, THAT MIGHT GIVE US SOME LEVERAGE . . .
MIGHT?!

NOW I'M SCARED! THE GHOSTS WERE JUST IRRITATING- CHAINS RATTLING, SHUTTERS SLAMMING- BUT THE GOVERNMENT! THEY CAN TAKE MY HOME AWAY- FREEZE MY ASSETS- ABSOLUTELY DESTROY SOMEONE ON HEARSAY!
MR. CURTIS- LET ME SHOW YOU WHERE I WANT YOU AND KIM TO WAIT WHILE BYRD AND I TALK TO THE BFD . . .
OH, JEFF . . .

FIRST IT WAS GHOSTS, THEN LAWSUITS, NOW A FEDERAL BUST! AND WHAT THIS WHOLE EXPERIENCE HAS DONE TO MY MARRIAGE . . .
FOR WHAT IT'S WORTH, KIM, I REALLY ADMIRE HOW STRONG YOU'VE BEEN THROUGH ALL THIS. YOU'RE IN FOR A BUMPY RIDE WHEN YOU FILE FOR DIVORCE, BUT THINK OF IT AS A NEW BEGINNING . . .

THE DIVORCE ⁘SIGH⁘ WELL, YOU'RE RIGHT ABOUT A NEW BEGINNING . . .

-BUT TOM AND I AREN'T SPLITTING UP- WE JUST FOUND OUT THAT I'M PREGNANT!

UH . . . CONGRATULATIONS?
JEFF? WHAT IS IT? OH- I KNOW-

I SHOULD'VE MENTIONED IT EARLIER, BUT WITH ALL THE URGENCY OVER THE RAID . . .
SURE, SURE . . . WELL, LIKE I SAID, CONGRATULATIONS. I KNOW THIS IS WHAT YOU ALWAYS WANTED . . .
KIM . . .

. . . LET ME SHOW YOU WHERE WE HAVE TO WAIT. JEFF, YOUR PARTNER NEEDS YOU OUTSIDE. THE BFD'S AT THE DOOR . . .
OH, TOM, IT'S ALL HITTING THE FAN NOW!
I'LL SAY IT IS!

ARE YOU THE CURTISES?
WE'RE THEIR LAWYERS.
BFD
AND THERE'S NO NEED FOR BATTERING RAMS.
BFD

NO ONE TELLS ME HOW TO GAIN ENTRANCE. STEP ASIDE OR I'LL HAVE YOU ARRESTED FOR OBSTRUCTION OF JUSTICE!
MY CLIENTS ARE MORE THAN WILLING TO GIVE YOU ENTRY-

--BUT YOU'LL HAVE TO TO EXECUTE THESE RELEASES.
WHAT THE HELL IS THIS?!

YOU SEE, WHEN THE MOON IS FULL-
BFD

-TOM AND KIM CURTIS'S HOME IS TRANSFORMED-
BFD

-AND THEY HAVE NO CONTROL OF THEIR HOUSE!
BFD

JEEZ!
WHA-
HOLEEE . . . !
@#*!?!
DON'T BELIEVE YOUR EYES, MEN-
THIS PLACE IS PROBABLY SO DRUG INFESTED, THE FUMES ARE MAKING US HALLUCINATE!

DRUGS AREN'T DOING THAT- THE FULL MOON IS! READ THE RELEASE- OR HAVE SOMEONE READ IT TO YOU- YOU'RE ABOUT TO TAMPER WITH THE UNKNOWN-
-AND MY CLIENTS DON'T WANT TO BE RESPONSIBLE!
ARE YOU DENYING ME ENTRANCE? SERGEANT!

CUFF 'EM!
I'M TELLING YOU- WE HAD THE HOUSE TESTED- THERE ARE NO DRUGS IN THERE!
THE WORST YOU'LL FIND IS EYE OF NEWT IN THE BUBBLING CAULDRON-- OUCH!
PIPE DOWN, CHUBBY

SURROUND THE HOUSE! BRING IN THE *DOGS*-
MOVE IT! MOVE IT!
CAPTAIN? THE DOGS DON'T WANT TO COME IN- THEY ACT LIKE THEY'RE *FRIGHTENED!*

WHEW! WHATTA *DUMP!*
JUNKIES- PUSHERS- THEY ALL LIVE LIKE *PIGS!*
HEY--WHAT'S THAT-- ?
SAY-- YOU BOYS FROM THE *GOVERNMENT?*

I'VE GOT A *BONE* TO PICK WITH YOU!

AIEEEEE!!

THAT AIN'T NO HALLUCINATION!
I KNOW WHAT I SAW!
I'M ONLY A DRUG ENFORCEMENT AGENT! MY JOB DESCRIPTION SAYS NOTHING ABOUT GHOSTS!
GOD, I LOVE IT WHEN I'M PROVEN RIGHT!
WOLFF! LOOK WHAT JUST APPEARED OUT OF NOWHERE!
H-HONEY? I'M SCARED . . . !
WATCH WHAT YOU SAY, KIM WE'RE LIVE!
AND INDEED THEY ARE, FOR IN THE WEEKS THAT FOLLOW . . .
ROOM WITH A DEJA VU
ILL- MANOR
A COUPLE COPES WITH AN OCCULTIST'S CURSE
Reno Scares Up Answers on BFD Snafu
The House with PMS
TONIGHT ON PAGE ONE WE TAKE A LOOK AT THE SORCERER WHO COMES IN AND REDECORATES A YOUNG COUPLE'S HOME ONCE A MONTH . . .
THE HOUSE THAT JACK BUILT- AND CAME BACK TO
When is a house not a home? Next on Donahue.
BFD TACTICS BOO'D
BAD HOUSEKEEPING!
Tom and Kim Curtis and Evil Roomers
FINALLY, ABOUT A MONTH LATER . . .
WHAT A MONTH! THE SETTLEMENT CHECK WE GOT FROM THE GOVERNMENT WAS ABLE TO PAY FOR THE REPAIRS- BUT HOW DID YOU GET THEM TO PAY SO FAST?
WITH ALL THE PRESS YOUR CASE HAS BEEN GETTING, THE BFD WANTED TO PUT THIS BEHIND THEM ASAP!
SINCE WE WERE ABLE TO GET A SETTLEMENT, I DECIDED NOT TO PRESS CHARGES FOR WRONGFUL ARREST
ANYWAY, YOU GOT ENOUGH MONEY TO COVER THE LAWSUITS AND SET UP YOUR OWN BUSINESS . . .
-AND ENOUGH TO SOCK AWAY FOR THE BABY!

BUT WHAT ABOUT MY NEW BUSINESS? THIS IS THE SECOND NIGHT OF THE FULL MOON- AND THE HOUSE *HASN'T* CHANGED!
I HAD TO CHANGE MY *SPIEL!*
CYPRESS SAID HE WOULDN'T REST UNTIL HE WAS ACKNOLWEDGED AS A LEGIT *OCCULTIST* . . . AND WITH THE *MEDIA* FOCUSING ON THE HOUSE FOR THE PAST MONTH-

-I'D SAY HIS 15 MINUTES OF FAME WAS ENOUGH TO LAST FOR ETERNITY!
JEFF--IT'S BEEN A HECTIC MONTH, BUT- I CAN'T THANK YOU ENOUGH, INCLUDING *SAVING MY MARRIAGE!*
ME?

SURE- I THINK TOM WAS GETTING A LITTLE *JEALOUS* . . . WHEN I WASN'T ON THE PHONE WITH YOU, I'D BE TELLING HIM ABOUT THE GREAT TIMES WE USED TO HAVE . . .
REALLY?

I THINK HE WAS AFRAID I'D CALL *CHASE HAWKINS* NEXT TO TALK ABOUT OLD TIMES! -AND WHO KNOWS WHERE THAT WOULD LEAD--REMEMBER HOW HE USED TO FLIRT WITH ME?
SIGH I SURE DO . . .
KIM!

EXCUSE US, COUNSELORS, WE'RE IN THE *HAUNTED HOUSE BUSINESS,* NOW!
GOOD LUCK, GUYS . . !
THE *TOURISTS* ARE HERE!

YES, THIS LOOKS LIKE A NORMAL HOUSE, BUT WE'LL TELL YOU-- SHOW YOU--HOW IT WAS POSSESSED BY A MAN NAMED JACK CYPRESS . . .
STEP RIGHT UP . . . $5, PLEASE- THANK YOU. CHILDREN UNDER 12, $3.50 . . .
HOW ARE YOU DOING, PARTNER?
AS ANOTHER WOLFE ONCE SAID- *"YOU CAN'T GO HOME AGAIN"* . . .
Tours Today!
AUTHENTIC HAUNTED HOUSE!
You've Seen Them on TV- Tom and Kim Curtis, Curators

END

WOLFF & BYRD
COUNSELORS OF THE
MACABRE
LADIES AND GENTLEMEN, ARE YOU BIASED IN ANY WAY TOWARDS THE SUPERNATURAL?

ALL I ASK OF THE JURY IS TO FAIRLY TRY THE CASE ON THE BASIS OF THE EVIDENCE AND NOT ON THE BASIS OF THE DEFENDANT'S APPEARANCE

YOUR HONOR! PLEASE TELL THE DEFENDANT TO REFRAIN FROM MAKING GESTURES TO THE POTENTIAL JURORS.
"MAKING GESTURES"?

THE PROSECUTOR IS TRYING TO WEEDLE MY CLIENT INTO CONTEMPT, YOUR HONOR
I WANT TO SEE YOU TWO AT THE BENCH- NOW!

UH- DID I DO SOMETHING WRONG, MR. BYRD?
WELL, WE'RE SELECTING THOSE PEOPLE TO BE YOUR JURY, NOT YOUR FRIENDS, SODD

MS. WOLFF, INSTRUCT YOUR CLIENT THAT THE ONLY WAIVING I'M GOING TO ALLOW IS FROM ATTORNEYS. GOT THAT?
YES, YOUR HONOR

MR. BYRD, I DON'T LIKE THE WAY THE PROSECUTOR'S ASSISTANT IS LOOKING AT ME . . .
BOYER? IGNORE HIM, SODD--I'M MORE CONCERNED WITH HOW THE JURORS LOOK AT YOU!

I DON'T LIKE THE WAY THAT THING'S LOOKING AT ME . . .
OH, WHY DID LARSON HAVE TO ENLIST ME AS SECOND CHAIR? I'D RATHER BE WORKING WITH BARKSDALE ON THAT TAX FRAUD CASE!

AS FOR YOU, MR. LARSON, I DON'T LIKE HISTRIONICS IN MY COURTROOM FROM THE DEFENSE OR THE PROSECUTION- UNDERSTAND?
UNDERSTOOD, JUDGE CHAMBERS

LET'S MOVE ON . . . EH? SIR--YEAH, YOU BACK THERE . . .
YOU COMING OR GOING? EITHER TAKE A SEAT OR GET OUT!
YOU HEARD THE JUDGE, FELLA

I THOUGHT THIS WAS JUDGE WYCOFF'S COURTROOM-- I GOTTA SHOW HIS CLERK I PAID MY FINE
JUDGE WYCOFF WON'T BE BACK TILL TOMORROW--HE'S LETTING JUDGE CHAMBERS USE HIS COURTROOM TODAY

JUDGE CHAMBERS' COURTROOM IS STILL BEING *CLEANED*- WOLFF AND BYRD'S CLIENT LEFT A LOT OF *FUNGUS* IN THERE!
DID YOU SAY WOLFF AND BYRD?

@#%~+*?!

THOSE @#%~+*?! LAWYERS WILL *HAUNT* ME TILL THE DAY *I* DIE!

NEED A *DRINK*...
SOMETHING *SWEET*...
...BUT *STIFF!*
VADE'S HAITIAN HUT
VADE'S HAITIAN HUT

..BUT IT'S TOO LATE
TO SAY YOU'RE SORRY
HOW WOULD I KNOW
HOW WOULD I CARE

YOU SERVE *ZOMBIES?*
WE SERVE *ANYBODY!* HYUK! WHATYA HAVE?

WHAT'S *THAT* SUPPOSED TO MEAN?
WHOA! DOWN BWAH! I WAS ONLY *KIDDING!*

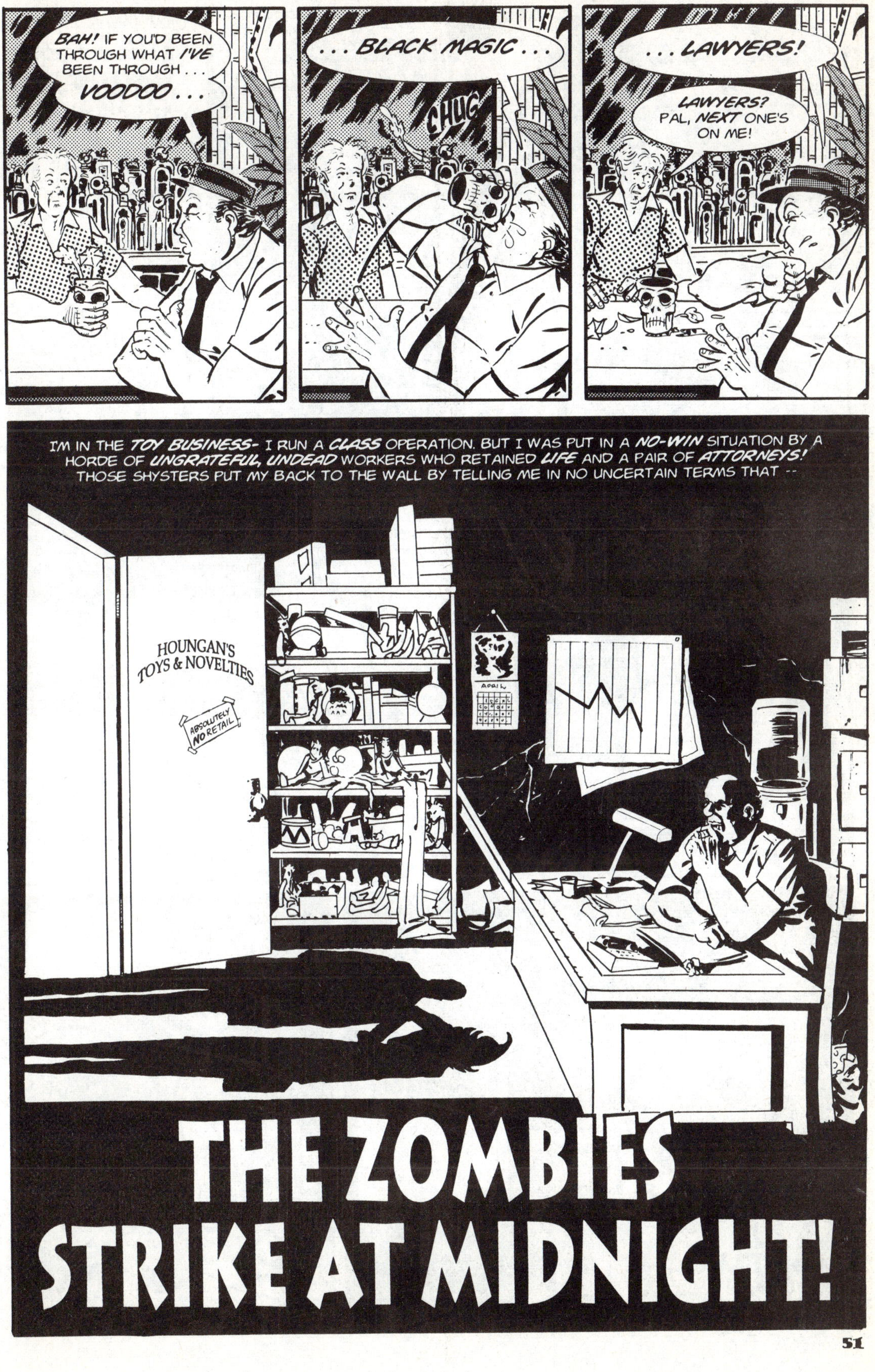

I'M IN THE *TOY BUSINESS*- I RUN A *CLASS* OPERATION. BUT I WAS PUT IN A *NO-WIN* SITUATION BY A HORDE OF *UNGRATEFUL, UNDEAD* WORKERS WHO RETAINED *LIFE* AND A PAIR OF *ATTORNEYS!* THOSE SHYSTERS PUT MY BACK TO THE WALL BY TELLING ME IN NO UNCERTAIN TERMS THAT --

HOUNGAN'S
TOYS & NOVELTIES

ABSOLUTELY NO RETAIL

THE ZOMBIES STRIKE AT MIDNIGHT!

"ATTORNEYS GIVE ME THE *CREEPS*, Y'KNOW? YA NEVER KNOW *WHAT* THEY GOT IN THEIR *BRIEFCASES* . . .

"HERE I AM EXPECTIN' A *WARRANT* OR SOMETHING, BUT THIS LAWYER REACHES IN AND PULLS OUT--

"ONE OF *MY VOODOO DOLLS!*

"THESE TWO EXPLAIN TO ME THAT THEY REPRESENT CLIENTS IN SUPERNATURAL MATTERS, YADDA YADDA . . . I SAYS, *SO?*
"I TELL 'EM I DON'T MAKE *REAL* VOODOO DOLLS, THEY'RE *TOYS!*"

OH, YEAH-- I'VE SEEN THEM AT *TOYS 'R' US!* YOU MAKE THEM?
IN A WAY-- BUT WITH-OUT THE LABEL, CAPICHE?
'NOTHER ROUND, WADE

"BUT THERE IS SOMETHING TO BE SAID ABOUT THAT VOODOO STUFF! I'VE DABBLED IN THE *BLACK ARTS*-- IF YOU KNOW *HOW* TO USE IT, YOU CAN GET *EFFICIENCY PLUS* FROM YER WORKERS!
OFFICIAL
"OKAY, SO I SAPPED THEIR *WILLS*-- BUT AT LEAST I WAS *PAYIN'* 'EM!

"SO THESE LAWYERS GET WIND OF MY SETUP AND START IN WIT' WORKING CONDTIONS, MINIMUM WAGE, AND GUARANTEED LIFE-TIME CONTRACTS. CAN YOU BELIEVE IT? FOR A *ZOMBIE?* THEY HADDA BE KIDDING. THERE WAS A *LADY LAWYER*-- GEEZ, A REAL *COLD FISH*-- THAT WAS REALLY BUSTIN' MY COJONES. I TOLD HER AN' HER LITTLE WUSS PARTNER TO GET THE HELL OUT . . .

"AND THAT'S WHEN SHE TOLD *ME* TA LOOK OUT THE WINDA--- *JEEZUS*, WHAT I SAW ALMOST MADE ME *PUKE!*"

"AS THE CLOCK STRUCK 12, MY ZOMBIE CREW WAS CIRCLING THE FACTORY-- I HEARD HOSTILE GROWLS -- SAW BLANK STARES -- WATCHED THEIR TIRELESS PACING --
HOUNGAN'S TOYS & NOVELTIES
UNFAIR
PAY THE VOO-DUES...
...PAY THE VOO-DUES...
PAY THE VOO-DUES...
ON STRI
UNFAIR TO UNDEAD
NO CONTRACT NO WORK!
..PAY THE VOO-DUES,
VOODOO DOLLARS IS PIN MONEY
"AND THE DAMNED CHANTING! IT WAS ENOUGH TO WAKE THE DEAD!"

AS IF THAT'S NOT BAD ENOUGH, THOSE @#%-+*?! LAWYERS SICKED THE STATE WAGE AND HOUR DIVISION ON ME! AND THEY PUT A LIEN FOR BACK PAY ON MY FACTORY!
ONE MORE, WADE HIC
THREE ZOMBIES IS THE LIMIT, BUD! COME UP FOR AIR WHILE I TEND TO THE OTHER CUSTOMERS . . .

SORRY, FOLKS, BUT I GOT CAUGHT UP LISTENING TO SOMEONE WHO STILL BELIEVES IN VOODOO ECONOMICS . . . SO WHAT'LL IT BE?

YOU SERVE ZOMBIES?
PRIESTS
PRIESTESSES
UNFAIR
NO CONTRACT NO WORK!
UNF

SO MUCH FOR HAPPY HOUR . . .!
PLOP!

LET HIM SLEEP IT OFF, FOLKS. AND BY THE WAY, THREE ZOMBIES IS THE SERVING LIMIT . . . !
WADE'S HAITIAN HUT
SEEING HOUNGAN POKE HIS HEAD IN HERE TODAY REMINDS ME THAT I SHOULD CALL THE ACCOUNTANT TO SEE IF HE'S TOTALLED THE BACK WAGE CLAIMS SO WE CAN COMPLETE OUR FILING!
HOUNGAN MAY HAVE HAD CONTROL OF THOSE ZOMBIES- BUT IT'S THE STATE'S FINES THAT ARE GOING TO EAT HIM ALIVE!

WITH JURY SELECTION OVER FOR THE DAY, ALANNA WOLFF, JEFF BYRD, AND THEIR CLIENT ARE CONFRONTED BY THE *JUDGE, JURY,* AND *EXECUTIONERS* OF THE . . .

COURT OF PUBLIC OPINION!

AKK! REPORTERS!

MS. WOLFF!

MR. BYRD!

IT'S ODD, THE IT THAT'S A THING!

ABOUT THE JURY SELECTION--!

THAT'S SODD

ARE ENVIRONMENTALISTS REPRESENTED ON THE JURY?

DOES THE CHANGING OF THE *SEASON* AFFECT YOUR CLIENT?

-STATE?
HE'S WITH SUPERMODEL DAWN DEVINE!
MS. DEVINE!
MR. HAWKINS!
CHASE! CHASE! CHASE!
DAWN! DAWN! DAWN!

HMPH-- THIS IS THE LAST TIME I GIVE THEM AN EXCLUSIVE!
CAN'T UNDERSTAND IT, PARTNER. TELLING THE PRESS WE PLAN TO WIN THE CASE FOR OUR CLIENT HAS TO BE THE BIGGEST SCOOP SINCE DOG BITES MAN!
TCH! JUST LOOK AT THOSE VULTURES!

MS. DEVINE, WHY ARE YOU BREAKING YOUR CONTRACT WITH THE GREATBODY AGENCY?
MR. HAWKINS, DOES GREATBODY HAVE AN INJUNCTION TO PREVENT HER FROM WORKING?
CHASE, WORD HAS IT YOU AND MS. DEVINE ARE AN ITEM-- ANY COMMENT?
OH! SO MANY QUESTIONS . . . CHASE, HONEY . . . ?
OKAY, KIDS, MS. DEVINE'S HAD A LONG DAY. I'LL GIVE YOU A STATEMENT . . .

I'M CONFIDENT THE JUDGE WILL RULE AGAINST THE OPPRESSIVE GREATBODY AGENCY-- LEAVING MS. DEVINE TO GO WITH WHOM-EVER SHE DESIRES!
ALL I DESIRE IS MY ATTORNEY!
CHASE, IS THERE A CHANCE MS. DEVINE WILL BECOME MRS. HAWKINS NUMBER FOUR?
WOW!
WHEN DID THIS START?
ISN'T THIS A CONFLICT OF INTEREST, MR. HAWKINS?
CAN WE GET A PICTURE?
YOU LUCKED OUT, SODD- YOU WERE ABLE TO BRUSH OFF THE PRESS!

YOU MEAN THEY BRUSHED *ME* OFF! WHAT AM *I*, *BUSH* LEAGUE?
SODD, YOU *WITHER* WHENEVER YOU SEE REPORTERS!

YOU SAID THE PRESS WAS *OFFENSIVE* BECAUSE THEY WERE TRYING TO DIG UP *DIRT* ON YOU!
WHO WOULD WANT TO READ ABOUT SOME BIMBO MODEL'S CONTRACT? *MY* CASE IS *NEWS*-- HER CASE IS *GOSSIP!*

SODD, YOU ACT LIKE THE MEDIA *KNOWS* THE DIFFERENCE-- *HEY!*
SODD! WHERE ARE YOU *GOING?*
TWIP
TWIP
TWIP
THEY *WANT* NEWS?

I'LL *GIVE* THEM NEWS!
I HOPE SODD DOESN'T DO ANYTHING *RASH*-- LIKE HIRING A *PUBLICIST!*
I KNOW-- HE CAN BARELY *AFFORD* HIS *LEGAL BILLS!*
FRANKLY, WOLFF, SODD DOES HAVE A *POINT* . . .

IT WOULDN'T HURT *US* TO GET SOME PUBLICITY. YOU'D THINK THERE'D BE MORE INTEREST, WHAT WITH OUR CLIENTELE
COME ON, BYRD-- WE GOT PLENTY OF COVERAGE OVER THE SUMMER WITH THE CURSE OF THE WERE-HOUSE SUIT. ANYWAY, THE MEDIA LOVES THE *FALLEN IDOL*-- WHETHER IT'S A SUPERMODEL, ROCK STAR, OR ATHLETE . . .

O. J.: COMPLETE COVERAGE
YEAH, BUT THERE IS SUCH A THING AS *OVERKILL* . . .!
IT'LL BE YESTERDAY'S NEWS BEFORE YOU KNOW IT, BYRD.
LET'S GO BACK TO THE OFFICE-- I DON'T LIKE LEAVING *MAVIS* THERE ALONE AFTER *DUSK* . . .

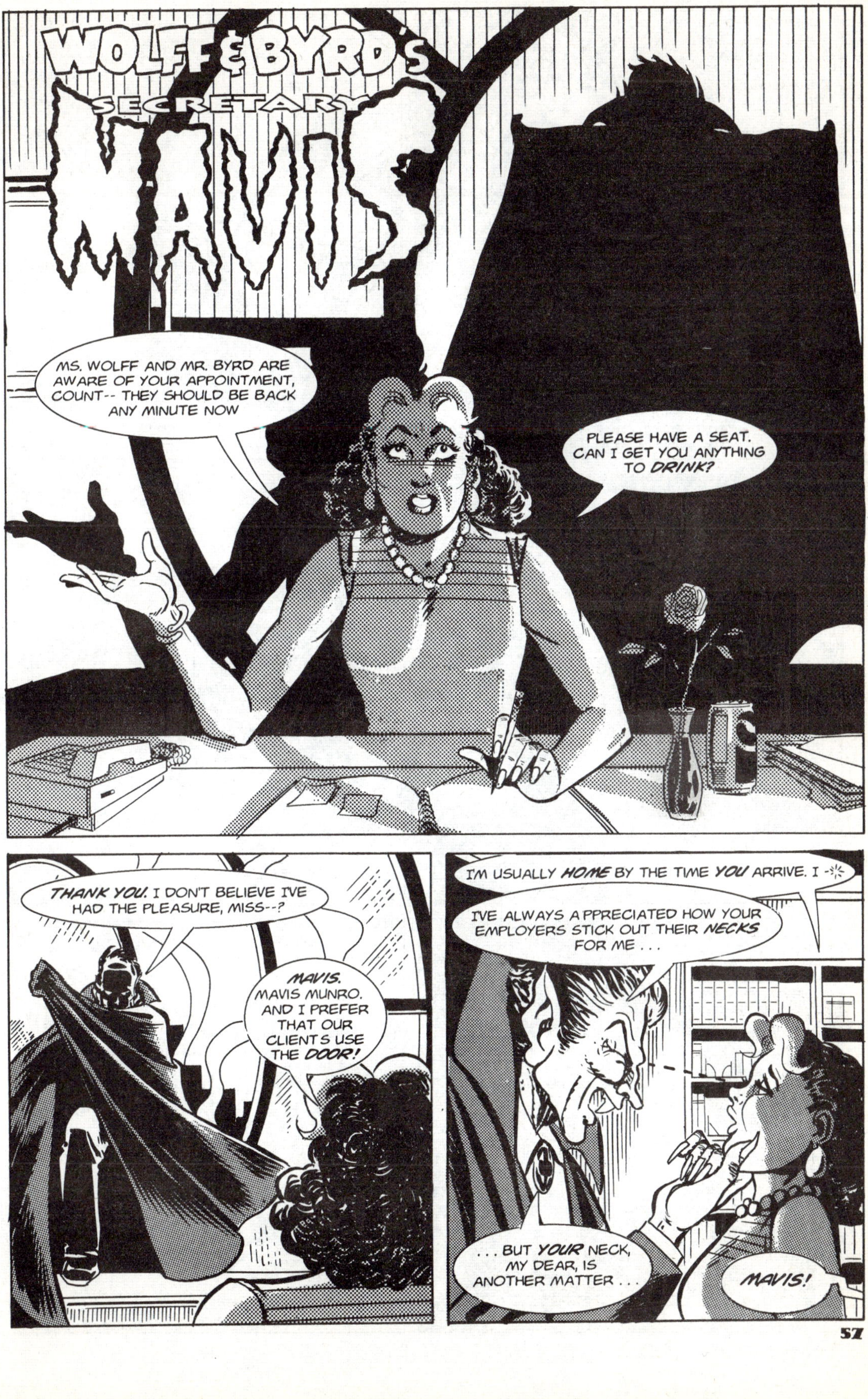

WOLFF & BYRD'S SECRETARY MAVIS

MS. WOLFF AND MR. BYRD ARE AWARE OF YOUR APPOINTMENT, COUNT-- THEY SHOULD BE BACK ANY MINUTE NOW

PLEASE HAVE A SEAT. CAN I GET YOU ANYTHING TO *DRINK?*

COUNT, WHY DON'T YOU WAIT IN THE CONFERENCE ROOM? WE WANT TO PREPARE YOU FOR WHEN THE PROSECUTOR CALLS YOU TO THE STAND . . .
YOU MEAN-THE CROSS-EXAMINATION? HSSS!

ARE YOU ALL RIGHT, MAVIS? COUNT TO TEN AND BREATHE DEEP
OH YEAH-- COUNT! DEEP BREATHING!

MAVIS, WHY DON'T YOU CALL IT A NIGHT? BYRD AND I CAN HANDLE THINGS NOW. I'LL CALL A CAR FOR YOU . . .
I'LL BE OKAY, MS. WOLFF! I'D RATHER WALK- THE NIGHT AIR WILL DO ME GOOD!
. . . THEY SAY I HUFFED, I SAY I PUFFED-- WHAT DIFFERENCE DOES IT MAKE? I COULDN'T HAVE BLOWN THAT DOOR DOWN! NOW THOSE GREEDY PIGS WANT TO SUE!
SORRY ABOUT THE DROOL, MR. BYRD
NO PROBLEM, MR. HOWELL

YOU SURE YOU DON'T WANT ME TO CALL A CAR? IT GETS A LITTLE HAIRY IN THIS NEIGHBORHOOD AFTER DARK!
DON'T WORRY, MS. WOLFF! THE FULL MOON DOESN'T FAZE ME! SEE YOU MAÑANA!

SHEESH! YOU'D THINK AFTER DEALING WITH HER CLIENTELE MS. WOLFF WOULD KNOW I'M NOT EASILY STARTLED--
OH!

GOTCHA! THIS BUM WAS PROBABLY WAITING FOR EVERY-ONE TO GO HOME SO HE COULD SLEEP IN THE BUILDING!
I'LL SEE TO IT THAT HE'S ESCORTED OUT, MS. MUNRO

OH- YOU SHOULD USE THE FREIGHT, MS. MUNRO-- THAT ELEVATOR'S BEEN GETTING STUCK BETWEEN FLOORS ALL DAY
I'LL TAKE MY CHANCES, RON. THANKS ANYWAY . . .
OK-- DON'T SAY I DIDN'T WARN YOU! LET'S GO, YOU

CLOSE TO A HALF HOUR LATER, WHEN MAVIS FINNALLY GETS TO STREET LEVEL . . .
GROAN WHY DIDN'T I LISTEN TO RON? I WISH I'D HAD A NEWSPAPER WHILE I WAS WAITNG FOR THAT @#-+*! ELEVATOR TO MOVE!
HMM- I SHOULD GET THIS ANYWAY- I'VE GOT TO READ ABOUT DAWN DEVINE LEAVING HER AGENCY!
POPULATION EXPLOSION FALSE ALARM
NOT ENOUGH PEOPLE?
LISA MARIE
BUSY BODY
SPECIAL FEATURE: WHAT'S BAD FOR YOU NOW
DON'T GET OUT OF BED
ASPCA BOYCOTTS 101 DALMATIONS
WE'RE NOT AGAINST CENSORSHIP, BUT...
50¢ CANDY NOW 55¢
PEOPL
SUZANNE SOMMERS ON HEALTH CARE, THE ECONOMY AND THIGHMAST

WALK
DONT WALK
YO!
WOO! WOO! WOO!
BABEEE!
MAMA!
UH OH-- I'LL CROSS HERE-- I WANNA AVOID BEING HIT ON . . .

WALK
HONK! HONK!
SCCRRREEEECCH!

HEY @*#@!! I'VE GOT THE LIGHT!
OKAY! OKAY! LET ME PICK UP MY--
TAXI

STOP THAT @*#@! HE STOLE MY PURSE! WHY DIDN'T YOU STOP HIM?!!
OH, GET THE HELL OUTTA MY WAY!
HUH? YEEOUCH!!

HONK!
ALL RIGHT ALREADY! I'M MOVING!

I'D BETTER TAKE THE SUBWAY SO I CAN GET RIGHT HOME-- IF I MAKE IT OFF THIS STREET IN ONE PIECE!
SMOKE SMOKE
SENS SENS
SMOKE SMOKE

WELL, HELLLO, SWEETHEART!

MAVIS?
CHANGED MY MIND, MS. WOLFF-- I'D RATHER WAIT UP HERE FOR A CAR SERVICE AND TAKE MY CHANCES WITH YOUR MONSTERS!

THINGS THAT GO BUMP IN THE NIGHT ...AND DAY!
LONG AFTER MAVIS GETS HER RIDE HOME, HER EMPLOYERS ARE STILL AT THE OFFICE, CATCHING UP ON THEIR CASELOAD...
WE SHOULD BE ABLE TO WRAP UP SODD'S JURY SELECTION BY TOMORROW...
OH, YEAH- THE JUDGE ISN'T GOING TO ACCEPT BOTANOPHOBIA AS A REASON FOR BEING DISMISSED ANYMORE
SAY, WOLFF-- HAVE YOU SEEN WHERE THE TRANSLATION IS FOR THIS SCROLL?
COURT

I CAN'T READ THIS-- I HAVE ENOUGH TROUBLE WITH LATIN LEGAL PHRASES, LET ALONE ANCIENT TIBETAN INCANTATIONS!
IT'S STILL IN THE COMPUTER, BYRD- MAVIS WAS GOING TO SPELL-CHECK IT
WE'RE NOT GOING TO TRIAL WITH THAT CASE. THE MUSEUM WANTS TO SETTLE
AND OUR CLIENT'S WILLING TO SETTLE?
OH, HE WAS UP IN THE AIR ABOUT IT, BUT HE FINALLY TOOK MY ADVICE TO GO WITH THE SETTLEMENT

I'M GOING TO CALL THE MUSEUM'S COUNSEL FIRST THING TOMORROW MORNING AND--
"TOMORROW" MORNING? CHECK IT OUT, WOLFF...

"PEOPLE TAKE SOLACE IN THE BELIEF THAT THE CREATURES OF THE NIGHT MUST RETURN AT DAWN TO THE SHADOWY WORLD THAT SPAWNED THEM . . .

BUT IT'S SO STEREOTYPICAL! SUPERNATURAL PHENOMENA FUNCTION 24 HOURS A DAY! THOUGH IT'S A SHAME THE MAJORITY OF OUR CLIENTS CAN'T ENJOY SUCH A PRETTY SIGHT . . . RIGHT, BYRD?

BYRD?

ZZZZZZ

SEVERAL HOURS LATER . . .
HOLA! MS. WOLFF? MR. BYRD? WELL! WHAT'S THIS?

Mavis-
Inform Mr. Byrd I went home to shower and sleep. Couldn't wait for him to catch his second wind. Remind him we must be at court by 10 a.m.
A. W.
P.S. Did you happen to catch the sunrise this morning?
BEE-YOO-TEE-FULL!

THE MAN WHO BROKE THE LAWS OF GRAVITY*

YOU'RE LATE! I GOT HERE ON TIME . . .

. . .AND I'VE BEEN UP ALL NIGHT, TOO!

*(AND LANDED IN COURT)

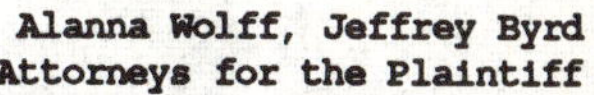

Alanna Wolff, Jeffrey Byrd
Attorneys for the Plaintiff

Professor Lowell M. Rose seeks compensation for personal injuries caused as result of gross negligence of Blackwood Museum (hereinafter, "the Defendant"). . . . Rose was hired to catalog artifacts, items, and papers for spring exhibition . . . Rose was told to translate ancient Tibetan scroll containing arcane incantations and spells . . . As Rose orally checked accuracy of ancient writ on levitation, Rose rose, finding himself hovering several feet above his desk. Buoyant at first, he was dismayed to learn he couldn't alight. . . . Defendant terminated Rose's employment, citing tampering with museum property and holding up the project . . . Rose requests court to regard his plight, as he now has no visible means of support . . . asks for punitive damages in amount of 20 million dollars, and ownership of Tibetan scrolls, to study for remedy . . .

Tobias J. Bascoe
Attorney for the Defendant

Plaintiff constantly looked down his nose at Blackwood Museum's owners, curators, other employees. . . . He was upset over not getting raise, even though Museum was employing him only for duration of exhibit . . . Plaintiff dabbled outside scope of his employment when he practiced spells inscribed on scrolls he was translating, resulting in his present state . . . Learning of Plaintiff's gravity-impaired condition, Museum was willing to work with Plaintiff, to monetary benefit of both. Plaintiff was apparently setting his sights high . . . demanded lofty position on Museum's board and pay scale that would escalate quarterly. . . . When Museum would not yield, Plaintiff filed suit . . . Museum fired him, since elevated physical condition put mystic artifacts exhibit behind schedule. . . .

OKAY, LET'S START WITH THE *PLAINTIFF* . . .
ARE YOU READY TO SETTLE, PROFESSOR ROSE?
ABSOLUTELY NOT!

I WANT TO GO TO TRIAL AND SUE THE MUSEUM!
YOU'LL HAVE TO SPEAK LOUDER, PROF. ROSE- THE COURT REPORTER CAN'T HEAR YOU
ER, JUDGE--?
PROFESSOR-!
YOUR HONOR, THIS IS OBVIOUSLY A PLOY . . . MY CLIENT HAS OFFERED THE PLAINTIFF A SIZABLE SETTLEMENT . . .

THIS IS JUST A HIGH-HANDED TACTIC TO GET MORE MONEY!
YOUR HONOR-?

-I REQUEST A RECESS SO I CAN SPEAK TO MY CLIENT- HE WENT OVER MY HEAD ON THIS
SIGH I'LL GIVE YOU A HALF-HOUR TO TALK SOME SENSE INTO HIM. . . IF THAT'S ALL RIGHT WITH MR. BASCOE
FINE WITH ME, YOUR HONOR

PRESENTLY . . .
WHAT'S THERE TO TALK ABOUT, MS. WOLFF? I WANT TO GO TO TRIAL!
I DON'T WANT TO DISCUSS THIS IN THE HALL-- LET'S GO INTO THE CONFERENCE ROOM

HEY, BOYER- LOOK! ANOTHER HIGH-PROFILE CLIENT FOR WOLFF AND BYRD! HYUK!
LARSON! WHATEVER THEIR CLIENT HAS MIGHT BE CONTAGIOUS! AND I DON'T WANT TO COME DOWN WITH IT!

THE AIR MUST BE GETTING THIN UP THERE, PROFESSOR. YOU REALIZE YOU CAN LOSE IN SUMMARY JUDGMENT--
--YOU WEREN'T REALLY AUTHORIZED TO TRY OUT THE SPELLS YOU WERE SUPPOSED TO BE CATALOGING!
I WANT MORE MONEY THAN THE MUSEUM'S OFFERING- AND I WANT TO BE AWARDED THE SCROLLS!
YOU HAVE TO SEE THINGS FROM MY PERSPECTIVE, COUNSELOR . . .

THOSE LOWBROWS AT THE MUSEUM WILL LET THE SCROLLS ROT IN AN ARCHIVE! I CAN USE THEM TO EXPAND MY MIND!
I'M ALREADY USING PURE BRAIN POWER TO LEVITATE . . . WHO KNOWS WHERE FURTHER STUDIES CAN TAKE ME?

AND REMEMBER-- I HIRED YOU-- AND YOU'LL DO AS I SAY. I WANT TO GO TO TRIAL!
FINE. IF THAT'S WHAT YOU WANT, LET'S GO TELL THE JUDGE
JUST EXPECT A LETTER FROM US THAT YOU'RE DOING THIS AGAINST OUR ADVICE . . .!

AND SO--
ALL RISE
HEH! YOU DON'T HAVE TO TELL ME
ALL RIGHT. HAS THE PLAINTIFF DECIDED TO SETTLE?
PROFESSOR . . . !
I'M SORRY, YOUR HONOR- BUT OUR CLIENT WANTS TO GO AHEAD WITH HIS SUIT . . .
HE DOES, DOES HE? WELL, I'LL GIVE YOU A RULING FROM THE BENCH-

I'M RULING IN FAVOR OF THE DEFENDANT'S MOTION--AND DISMISSING THE CASE
WHAT?!
THANK YOU, JUDGE
KLOP!

I WON'T STAND FOR THIS! I KNEW I WASN'T GOING TO GET A FAIR HEARING!
I WANT TO GO TO A HIGHER COURT- THIS TIME WITH A MALE JUDGE!
THAT DOES IT, MISTER!
I'M TAKING YOU OFF YOUR HIGH HORSE RIGHT NOW! BAILIFF! BRING HIM DOWN!

PROFESSOR- DON'T! YOU'RE FLEEING THE LAW!
BAH! THIS IS ALL BENEATH ME! I NEED TO BE OUT IN THE OPEN-- FREE TO BE AT ONE WITH THE UNIVERSE--

PROFESSOR! THAT'S A VERY HIGH THRESHOLD--
DON'T I KNOW IT, MS. WOLFF--TA TA! SEND ME YOUR BILL-- CARE OF THE COSMOS!

BONK!
OOOH--! I FELT THAT!
TSK I TRIED TO WARN HIM . . . !

SEVERAL DAYS LATER . . .
YOU WERE LUCKY YOU WERE KNOCKED OUT, PROFESSOR . . . AFTER YOU WERE TAKEN TO THE HOSPITAL, I WAS ABLE TO CONVINCE THE JUDGE NOT TO HOLD YOU IN CONTEMPT!

...AND SUING THE COURT IS A BAD IDEA. BESIDES, YOU INJURED THE BAILIFF WHEN YOU FELL--AND HE WAS IN THE COURSE OF PERFORMING HIS DUTIES . . .
IS THAT THE PROFESSOR? I'M SURE I GOT THIS STIFF NECK FROM LOOKING UP AT HIM!

AND SOMETHING MUST'VE HAPPENED WHEN I HIT MY HEAD, MS. WOLFF!
NO MATTER HOW HARD I CONCENTRATE, I CAN'T LEVITATE!
I'VE GOT TO BE ABLE TO SUE SOMEBODY! I WAS UP THERE--I COULD'VE BEEN TOP OF MY FIELD! NOW THE ONLY THING THAT'S RISING IS MY BLOOD PRESSURE!
THAT PATIENT WAS ABLE TO DEFY GRAVITY? HOW COULD THAT BE POSSIBLE, DOCTOR?
JUST LISTEN TO HIM, NURSE! HE'S OBVIOUSLY FULL OF HOT AIR!

END

A HOST OF HORRORS

I'M *BACK,* BOYS AND GHOULS!

YOU CAN'T KEEP A GOOD MANIAC DOWN!

THE BIER-MEISTER RETURNS WITH STORIES IN THAT OLD (CHOKE!) HORROR TRADITION!

COMING SOON TO THE EEK! CHANNEL

THE ALL-HORROR NETWORK

THE NETWORK OF FEAR

THIS PAST OCT. 31ST:
LAFAYETTE
GRISTLE'S MEATS
AN ALL-HORROR NETWORK? HAS ANYONE THOUGHT THAT CHILDREN MIGHT TUNE IN?
I'M NOT FAMILIAR WITH THE HORROR GENRE, JOSETTE, BUT I RECALL READING THAT IT TENDS TO BE VIOLENT AND MISOGYNISTIC . . .
I'M NOT FOR CENSORSHIP, BUT DO CHILDREN NEED TO BE EXPOSED TO SUCH NEGATIVITY?

I MEAN, LOOK HOW MORBID HALLOWEEN'S BECOME! SO MUCH DWELLING ON THE DARK SIDE-- A CHILD CAN'T HELP BUT BE INFLUENCED BY IT!
IT DOESN'T HELP WHEN KIDS SEE MORE AND MORE ADULTS DRESSING UP ON HALLOWEEN . . .

CHILDREN HAVE TROUBLE SEPARATING FANTASY FROM REALITY . . . PEOPLE HAVE TO BE MADE AWARE OF THIS!
WE CAN ONLY DO WHAT WE CAN TO MAKE THIS A MORE POSITIVE WORLD FOR THE CHILDREN TO GROW UP IN . . .

HEH . . . HEH . . . HEH . . .

FRYER'S CLUB DIS-MEMBERS ONLY
HEH!

HEH . . . HEH . . .
HEH . . . HEH . . .
HEH
WELL, HELLO, KIDDIES!
HEY, GANG! LOOK WHAT SLITHERED IN! OUR OLD PAL, THE BIER-MEISTER!
PULL UP A SLAB WITH YOUR OLD FIENDS . . .
NEVILLE THE BOOTBLACK . . .
GEORGIE . . .
THE FARMER IN THE HELL . . .
THE SPELUNKER OF THE SEPULCHERS . . .
THE DEATH OF THE PARTY . . .
AND YOURS TRULY, THE BIG CREEP!
YOU'RE JUST IN TIME TO SWAP SOME TEPID TALES OF TERROR AND CHOP TALK!
WHERE HAVE YOU BEEN? YOU MISSED THE LAST FEW OF OUR MOTLEY MEETINGS!
DON'T WORRY, I HAVEN'T BEEN AVOIDING MY (UGH!) CADAVEROUS CONTEMPORARIES . . .
I HOPE NOT! WE UNEMPLOYED HORROR HOSTS HAVE TO (YECH!) STICK TOGETHER . . .
I'VE JUST BEEN BUSY PLANNING THE BIGGEST COMEBACK SINCE LAZARUS . . .
GIVE A GLAZED GAZE AT THIS GLIB GAZETTE AND GAG ON MY GREAT NEW GIG!
VARIETY

HEH . . . HEH . . . HEH . . .
HEH . . . HEH . . . HEH . . .

THE NEXT DAY . . .
LARSON, I KNOW WE HAVE A GOOD CASE AGAINST THIS SODD THING . . . BUT I DON'T THINK YOU SHOULD UNDERESTIMATE HIS ATTORNEYS . . .
THE FINAL JUDGMENT
Bar & Grill
WHY? BECAUSE I'VE NEVER WON A CASE DEFENDED BY WOLFF & BYRD?
PART 2
BAR ASSOCIATION
WOLFF AND BYRD WON THOSE CASES ON TECHNICALITIES, BOYER. YOU SEE HOW OUR HANDS ARE TIED WORKING FOR THE D.A. . . .
YEAH-- THEY DON'T LIKE IT WHEN WE BREAK THE RULES!
AREN'T THERE ANY BARS IN MANHATTAN, TOBY? WHY'D WE HAVE TO COME TO A LAWYERS' HANGOUT IN BROOKLYN FOR A DRINK?
WELL, DAN, THERE JUST HAPPENS TO BE A CERTAIN FEMALE LAWYER I WANT TO "ACCIDENTALLY" RUN INTO . . . AND DON'T CALL ME TOBY! IT'S TOBIAS!
THEY DON'T LIKE IT WHEN WE'RE CAUGHT BREAKING THE RULES. THERE'S A DIFFERENCE. BUT WE HAVE AN ADVANTAGE IN THE SODD CASE. ALANNA WOLFF IS ARGUING IT.
THAT'S AN ADVANTAGE? SHE'S SCARIER THAN HER CLIENT!
AH, BUT SHE'S A WOMAN, BOYER. AS YOU GET MORE TRIAL EXPERIENCE, YOU'LL LEARN THAT WOMEN ARE FAR MORE EMOTIONAL THAN MEN.
AH!

THAT'S WHY MEN MAKE BETTER LAYWERS-- WE'RE RATIONAL BY NATURE. IT'S A FACT. NOW, I DON'T MIND THAT THERE'S FEMALE ATTORNEYS-- SOMEONE LIKE WOLFF IS NICE TO LOOK AT.
THOUGH I'D PREFER THAT SHE HAD A LITTLE MORE MEAT ON HER BONES . . .
WELL FEAST YOUR EYES, LARSON-- LOOK WHO JUST WALKED IN . . .

SO, DO I GET MY BIRTHDAY DRINK TONIGHT, MR BYRD?
HEY, I WAS READY TO BUY YOU ONE YESTERDAY, MS. WOLFF-- IT'S NOT MY FAULT YOUR BIRTHDAY FALLS ON HALLOWEEN-- WHEN ALL OUR CLIENTS COME OUT!
HIYA, COUNSELORS! WHAT'LL YA HAVE?

SHE'S COMING THIS WAY! DUCK! MAYBE SHE WON'T SEE US!
OH, BOYER, IT IS AFTER HOURS . . . AND LAWYERING DOES MAKE STRANGE BEDFELLOWS (CHUCKLE) . . .

WELL, WELL, AS I LIVE AND BREATHE, ALANNA WOLFF
I THOUGHT THAT WAS YOU, LARSON. SAY, REMEMBER HOW YOU HAD ONE OF SODD'S LIMBS CUT OFF FOR EVIDENCE?
YEAH, SO?

WELL, I JUST FILED A SUIT IN FEDERAL COURT CLAIMING MY CLIENT'S CIVIL RIGHTS HAVE BEEN VIOLATED, AND WEVE NAMED YOU AS ONE OF THE DEFENDANTS!
PFFT!

HOW DARE SHE! SHE'S JUST GRANDSTANDING! SHE'S TRYING TO MUDDY THE WATER! INTIMIDATION DOESN'T WORK!
YOU HEAR THAT, ALANNA? #$%*! YOU CAN'T DO THIS TO ME! YOU'RE NOT GONNA GET A DIME OUTTA ME! #$%*! NOT A DIME!
L-LARSON! PLEASE! PULL YOURSELF TOGETHER! LET'S GET OUT OF HERE BEFORE YOU DO SOMETHING YOU'LL REGRET!
THAT'S HER, DAN! REMEMBER THAT CASE I SETTLED FOR THE MUSEUM ABOUT THE GUY WHO BROKE THE LAWS OF GRAVITY? SHE WAS HIS LAWYER!
ALANNA! CAUSING TROUBLE OVER THERE?
ME? NEVER!
WE'RE LEAVING-- I KNOW THESE ATTORNEYS AND I DON'T WANT TO BE HERE WHEN ONE OF THEIR CLIENTS SHOWS UP!
SHE'S GOT TO BE A FOOT TALLER AND TEN YEARS OLDER THAN YOU, TOBIAS! AND WHO'S HER HAIRDRESSER-- EDWARD SCISSORHANDS?

"L. L. PUBLISHING HAS SIGNED BEST-SELLING BRITISH HORROR NOVELIST *NILES PIB* TO WRITE A NON-FICTION ACCOUNT OF *REAL-LIFE* HORROR *SODD, THE THING CALLED IT.* SODD, WHOSE REAL NAME IS HERBERT MOSS, IS A FORMER CHEMICAL PLANT WORKER TRANSFORMED INTO AN EIGHT-FOOT MASS OF LIVING VEGETATION EARLIER THIS YEAR . . .

"A *GRAVE-ROBBING* INCIDENT OCCURRED EARLY THIS MORNING AT ST. WILLIAM'S CEMETERY. AFTER RESPONDING TO CALLS COMPLAINING OF LOUD NOISES COMING FROM THE CEMETERY, THE POLICE CAME UPON A WEIRD GANG HUDDLED OVER THE OPEN *GRAVE* OF *DR. FORREST BERTRUM*, A NOTED PSYCHIATRIST WHO DIED LAST YEAR. THE BODY WAS NOWHERE TO BE FOUND.

"THE BIER-MEISTER IS A *GHOUL* WHOSE CELEBRITY CAME 40 YEARS AGO AS A "HORROR HOST" WHO SPUN *VIOLENT* TALES OF THE *SUPERNATURAL* FOR PRIMARILY A *YOUNG* AUDIENCE. A GHOUL IS BELIEVED TO *FEAST* ON THE LIVING OR DEAD *FLESH* OF HUMANS. THE BIER-MEISTER CLAIMS TO BE A STRICT VEGETARIAN. . . .

"THE HORROR HOST PROFESSION SUFFERED A *SEVERE BLOW* IN THE *1950S* WHEN DR. BERTRUM RELEASED A STUDY *LINKING* HORROR STORIES TO *JUVENILE DELINQUENCY.* ALTHOUGH BERTRUM'S THEORIES WERE *NEVER* PROVEN, HE INFLUENCED PARENTS' GROUPS TO URGE *LEGISLATORS* TO PASS A LAW *BANNING* HORROR STORIES FOR ANYONE UNDER THE AGE OF 18. THE HORROR HOSTS CALLED IT QUITS *BEFORE* ANY SUCH LAW WAS PASSED . . .

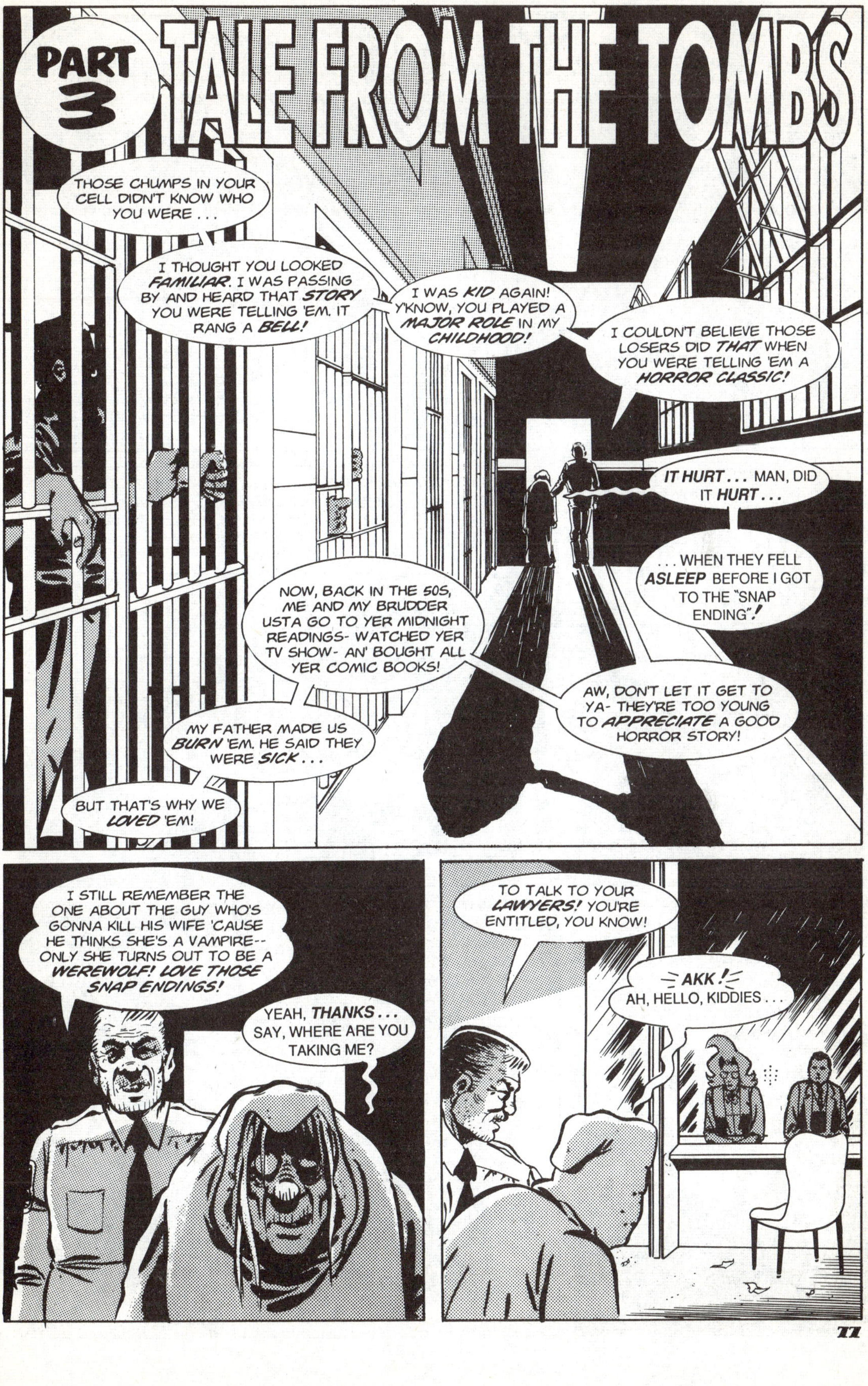

PART 3 TALE FROM THE TOMBS

THOSE CHUMPS IN YOUR CELL DIDN'T KNOW WHO YOU WERE . . .

I THOUGHT YOU LOOKED *FAMILIAR*. I WAS PASSING BY AND HEARD THAT *STORY* YOU WERE TELLING 'EM. IT RANG A *BELL!*

I WAS *KID* AGAIN! Y'KNOW, YOU PLAYED A *MAJOR ROLE* IN MY *CHILDHOOD!*

I COULDN'T BELIEVE THOSE LOSERS DID *THAT* WHEN YOU WERE TELLING 'EM A *HORROR CLASSIC!*

IT HURT . . . MAN, DID IT **HURT . . .**

. . . WHEN THEY FELL **ASLEEP** BEFORE I GOT TO THE "SNAP ENDING"**!**

NOW, BACK IN THE 50S, ME AND MY BRUDDER USTA GO TO YER MIDNIGHT READINGS- WATCHED YER TV SHOW- AN' BOUGHT ALL YER COMIC BOOKS!

MY FATHER MADE US *BURN* 'EM. HE SAID THEY WERE *SICK . . .*

BUT THAT'S WHY WE *LOVED* 'EM!

AW, DON'T LET IT GET TO YA- THEY'RE TOO YOUNG TO *APPRECIATE* A GOOD HORROR STORY!

OKAY, YOU **AXED** FOR IT! HERE'S MY TALE OF A NIGHT OUT WITH THE BOYS THAT TURNED OUT TO BE A

GRAVE MISTAKE!

"OKAY, OKAY! HERE'S THE **GIST** OF IT. ME AND THREE OTHER HORROR HOST HAS-BEENS WERE **DRUNK AS SKUNKS . . .** WE COULDN'T GET THE OTHER MEMBERS OF OUR CLUB TO COME WITH US TO PAY OUR **LAST RESPECTS** TO THE MAN WHO PUT US OUT OF A JOB-- **DR. FORREST BERTRUM . . .**

"I WAS CAUGHT OFF-GUARD . . . THE POLICEMAN'S FLASHLIGHT BLINDED ME AS I WAS HANDCUFFED. I COULD HEAR THE CACOPHONY OF BONES CLACKING INTO THE DISTANCE AS MY FELLOW FIENDS FLED . . . LEAVING ME TO SUFFER THE CONSEQUENCES, IN DIRE NEED OF A BATHROOM . . .

SO THAT'S MY STORY! THIS IS THE FIRST TIME I'M TELLING IT--'CAUSE THE COPS WOULDN'T LISTEN! INSTEAD, THEY READ ME A LITTLE DITTY THEY GOT FROM SOMEONE NAMED MIRANDA! SO WHAT HAPPENED TO BERTRUM? BEATS THE HELL OUTA ME! THIS GHOUL'S NO FOOL-- I KNOW GRAVE ROBBING'S A FELONY! I'M JUST WAITING FOR MY CREEPY COMRADES TO COME FORWARD TO GIVE THE AUTHORITIES AN ALIBI THEY'LL BUY SO I CAN WAVE THIS BRIG BYE-BYE!

BUT THEY HAVEN'T COME FORWARD, HAVE THEY?
UH . . . NO . . .
THEN LEAVE THIS TO YOUR ATTORNEYS, BIER - UH- MEISTER

BUT I REALLY CAN'T AFFORD TO HIRE YOU--
LET'S NOT WORRY ABOUT THAT NOW. OUR PRIORITY IS TO GET YOU OUT OF HERE
COURT IS READY TO CONVENE- WE HAVE TO TRANSFER THE PRISONER TO THE COURTROOM

OKAY, THEN. WE'LL BE UP THERE WITH YOU TO PLEAD YOUR CASE. IF WE HAVE TO, WE'LL GET BAIL POSTED FOR YOU.
I'D LIKE TO SEE JUSTICE SERVED-- BUT IF THE JUDGE IS COLD BLOODED, IT MIGHT BE JUST ICE! HEE-HEE! 'BYE NOW!
OY! THOSE PUNS!

GLAD YOU GOT MY MESSAGE, MS. WOLFF- I SHOULDA KNOWN THE BIER-MEISTER WAS ALREADY YOUR CLIENT. I WAS ABOUT TO GIVE THE OLD GHOUL A PUBLIC DEFENDER!
WE APPRECIATE IT, LEROY. LET'S JUST SAY WE'RE TAKING THIS ONE TO FULFILL OUR PRO BONO TIME . . .
WROTEN

HEH-HEH.! LEMME TELL YOU, THOSE ***SHOCK SHYSTERS*** MAY BE EXPENSIVE BUT THEY GOT MY ***INCARCERATED CARCASS*** OUT OF THE CLINK.! ALANNA AND JEFF WERE ABLE TO GET THE ***CABLE STATION*** (THE ONE AIRING MY ***SPECIAL***--CHECK YOUR LOCAL LISTINGS.!) TO ***POST BOND.!*** AND IT'S A ***GOOD*** THING, TOO-- IF I HAD TO SPEND ***ANOTHER*** NIGHT IN ***JAIL***-- (SHUDDER.!). WELL, GIVE ME A ***MAUSOLEUM*** ANYTIME.!.! SINCE I HAVE TO ***WAIT*** FOR MY ***APPOINTMENT*** WITH MY ***BRR-ARRISTERS,*** HOW ABOUT A LITTLE ***SCARE-STORY*** FROM MY ACHING ARCHIVES? YOU'VE PROBABLY HAD IT WITH ALL THE ***LEGAL MUMBO-JUMBO*** YOU HAVE TO WADE THROUGH-- LEMME TELL A GOOD HORROR STORY YOU CAN SINK YOUR ***TEETH*** INTO . . .

WOLFF & BYRD COUNSELORS OF THE MACABRE

. . . IN FACT, THAT'S THE PREDICAMENT OUR ***PARANOID PROTAGONIST*** FINDS HIMSELF IN WHEN HE THINKS HIS ***BLUSHING BRIDE*** IS A ***PAIN IN THE NECK . . .***

PART 4

UH- I GUESS YOU HEARD THAT ONE BEFORE...!
NO OFFENSE, BUT EVER SINCE I STARTED WORKING AS WOLFF AND BYRD'S SECRETARY, HORROR STORIES JUST DON'T DO IT FOR ME!

AHH, YOU DON'T KNOW HORROR! I'VE GOT THE REAL STUFF!
...YOU CAN LOOK AT DOCUMENTS AND FILINGS, MR. PIB. YOU CAN'T TALK TO SODD. PERIOD. I DON'T WANT YOU TO BE CALLED IN AS A WITNESS!
I WOULDN'T DREAM OF JEOPARDIZING SODD'S CASE, MS. WOLFF-- I'M JUST GOING TO BE AN OBSERVER! AND PLEASE-- CALL ME NILES!

SO THAT'S NILES PIB! HE WRITES THAT MYSTICAL JUNK THAT PASSES FOR HORROR TODAY!
EXCUSE ME--!

FEEL FREE TO CALL ME IF YOU HAVE ANY QUESTIONS WHILE YOU'RE WRITING YOUR BOOK, NILES...
UM, AH... I DIDN'T WANT TO BOTHER YOU BEFORE- BUT I'VE BEEN READING YOUR LATEST NOVEL AND... WELL...
COULD YOU SIGN IT?
WHY, I'D BE GLAD TO!

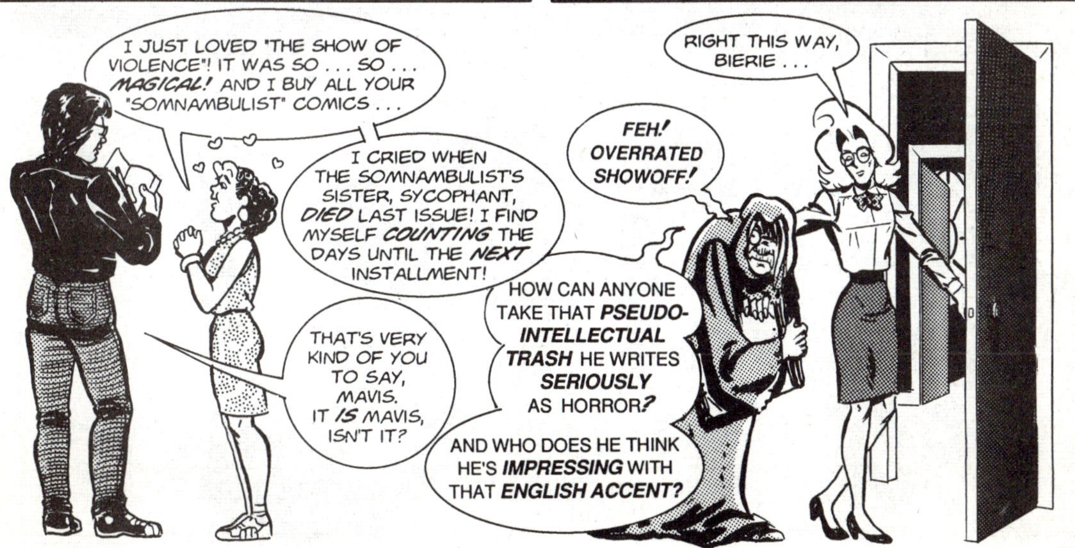

I JUST LOVED "THE SHOW OF VIOLENCE"! IT WAS SO... SO... MAGICAL! AND I BUY ALL YOUR "SOMNAMBULIST" COMICS...
I CRIED WHEN THE SOMNAMBULIST'S SISTER, SYCOPHANT, DIED LAST ISSUE! I FIND MYSELF COUNTING THE DAYS UNTIL THE NEXT INSTALLMENT!
THAT'S VERY KIND OF YOU TO SAY, MAVIS. IT IS MAVIS, ISN'T IT?
RIGHT THIS WAY, BIERIE...
FEH! OVERRATED SHOWOFF!
HOW CAN ANYONE TAKE THAT PSEUDO-INTELLECTUAL TRASH HE WRITES SERIOUSLY AS HORROR?
AND WHO DOES HE THINK HE'S IMPRESSING WITH THAT ENGLISH ACCENT?

. . . ANDHE'D BE LOST WITHOUT THAT COLLEGE FRESHMAN COFFEEHOUSE CROWD LAPPING UP THAT PAP HE WRITES!
AH, LET'S MOVE ON, OKAY? I'VE GOT GOOD NEWS. THE CHARGES AGAINST YOU HAVE BEEN DROPPED-
-AND MY PARTNER'S AT THE NETWORK ON YOUR BEHALF. IN THE MEANTIME, LET ME TELL YOU WHAT REALLY HAPPENED AT THE CEMETERY . . .

YOU SEE, SOME COLLEGE KIDS STOLE BERTRUM'S BODY SHORTLY BEFORE YOU AND YOUR GANG SHOWED UP.
THEY HAD LEARNED ABOUT BERTRUM'S CAMPAIGN AGAINST HORROR HOSTS IN THE 50S. DECIDING THAT WASN'T TOO COOL, THEY DUG HIM UP TO BE THEIR FRAT HOUSE'S HALLOWEEN HOST FOR THE NIGHT . . .
SOUNDS LIKE KIDS AFTER MY OWN HEART . . . NOT THAT I WANT TO GIVE THEM ANY IDEAS!

THEY WERE GOING TO SLIP THE BODY BACK BY MORNING, BUT THE RUCKUS YOUR GROUP MADE BROUGHT ATTENTION TO THE GRAVE! THE STUDENTS EVENTUALLY CONFESSED-- BESIDES, THEY WERE STUCK WITH A CORPSE!
WHEW! MY MOAN-AMIS WILL BE RELIEVED TO HEAR THIS!
BIERIE, YOUR FRIENDS HAVEN'T DONE ANYTHING TO HELP YOU. WHAT IF THOSE STUDENTS HAD NEVER CONFESSED? YOU WOULD BE TAKING THE RAP!
YEAH, WELL . . . I DON'T LIKE TO THINK THAT A LOT OF MY FELLOW SPINETINGLERS ARE JUST SPINELESS. LIKE IN THE 50s-- WE COULD'VE FOUGHT BERTRUM-- BUT EVERYONE WAS AFRAID TO SPEAK OUT.

SINCE THEN, BERTRUM'S BEEN OUR CONVENIENT BOOGEYMAN. WE BLAME HIM FOR ALL OUR FAILURES. I TELL MYSELF IT CAN'T HAPPEN AGAIN, BUT . . .
IT'S UP TO YOU AND YOUR PROFESSION, BIERIE. IF YOU ALLOW IT TO HAPPEN, IT WILL!
BYRD! HOW'D IT GO?
HAVE YOU SEEN THE PAPER TODAY, WOLFF?

WHY, NO-- I HAVEN'T HAD A CHANCE . . .
WELL, READ IT AND WEEP!

EEK! CHANNEL FEELS PRESSURE FROM LOCAL PARENTS' GROUP

COUPLE VOWS TO FIGHT HORROR-IBLE INFLUENCE ON KIDS

by Keith Michaels, *exclusive to the World Press*

A local parents' activist group today announced plans to go after the Eek Channel All-Horror Network that is supposed to debut on local cable systems this January. They say they were spurred to action by the recent grave-robbing incident in which the body of the late Dr. Forrest Bertram was removed from St. William's Cemetery.

Josette LaFargue, president and founder of the Children's Movement Activist Association (CMAA), decided to take action when she read that the students who pulled the Halloween prank were inspired by the old horror host, the Bier-Meister, who is slated to host a show on the upcoming EC network. "We have to protect our children from this type of media influence," she stated in a news conference here yesterday. "Obviously, such trash has reached over the decades to motivate these young people to commit such a ghastly crime."

A spokesperson for the EC Network has responded to the allegations of being a bad influence on children by stating, "We never meant any harm. It's just good clean fun," said Alice Feldstein. "We're currently deciding on various packages available from the studios to provide us with original programming. Meanwhile, we signed the Bier-Meister for a one-time special to help launch the network and give a nostalgic look back at the old era of horror programs. Of course, we wouldn't want to upset the parents too much, and we do plan to take a very close look at what the Bier-Meister plans to present on this special."

However, an insider at the horror network who requested anonymity has told the World Press that the EC Network has pushed back the Bier-Meister's special and is considering shelving the project if the CMAA pressure mounts.

Josette (left) and Gershon (right) LaFargue are heads of the Children's Movement Activist Association (CMAA), whose goal is to protect children from what they consider to be negative influences in the media. (Photo by S. Rampart)

SUPERMODEL ORDERED BACK TO WORK

First Round with Greatbody Agency

TWO WEEKS LATER
COUNSELORS, I'M A WRECK! I KNOW WE SHOULD FIGHT THE CMAA BUT . . .
IT WOULD BE NICE TO HAVE YOUR FELLOW HORROR HOSTS SUPPORTING YOU ON THIS, RIGHT?
CAN YOU BELIEVE IT, JEFF? THOSE YELLOW-BELLIED BLOWHARDS ARE MAD AT ME! THEY SAY I'M JUST MAKING THINGS WORSE AND WE'LL LOSE WHAT LITTLE WE'VE GOT NOW!
THEY'RE WRONG, BIERIE! THE COUNTY'S BANNING OF THE HORROR NETWORK THAT PLANNED TO AIR YOUR SHOW VIOLATES THE NETWORK'S AND YOUR FIRST AMENDMENT RIGHTS!
PART 5
TESTIMONY CALCULATED TO DRIVE YOU MAD!
YOU DID THE RIGHT THING, BIERIE-- WE PRESENTED OUR CASE. ALL WE CAN DO NOW IS WAIT UNTIL JUDGE DEWEY'S RULING . . .
BUT SOME OF THE STUFF THAT WAS SAID IN COURT . . . WAS THAT EXPERT WITNESS FOR REAL?
DR. HENNINGS, IN YOUR EXPERT OPINION, IN WHAT WAY DO HORROR STORIES HAVE A HARMFUL EFFECT ON CHILDREN?
AS SENIOR PSYCHIATRIST AT RINEHART HOSPITAL, I'VE SEEN CASE STUDIES OF CHILDREN WHO HAVE HAD CONTINUED EXPOSURE TO HORROR MOVIES . . .
THEY LAUGH AT THEM.
OUR STUDY CONCLUDED THAT HORROR STORIES OBVIOUSLY DESENSITIZE CHILDREN. IT MAY HAPPEN TO ONE CHILD OUT OF A THOUSAND . . .
. . . BUT THAT'S ONE CHILD TOO MANY!
WHEW- AND I THOUGHT MY STORIES WERE FAR-FETCHED!
HEY, THIS IS THE 90s, BIER-MEISTER! TRUST ME, OPINIONS MORE IDIOTIC THAN DR. HENNINGS' HAVE BEEN ACCEPTED BY THE COURT!
THERE'S THE CMAA GANG-- AND DON'T THEY LOOK SMUG!

WE DID OUR PART. NOW IT'S UP TO THE JUDGE . . .
:CHUCKLE: I HEARD HIS NICKNAME IS "THE HANGING JUDGE"!
I HAVE A GOOD FEELING ABOUT THIS- I FEEL IT IN MY BONES!
YOU HANDLED YOURSELF VERY WELL ON THE STAND, DR. HENNINGS . . .
THE FACTS ARE ON OUR SIDE, GERSHON. YOU CAN TELL THE OTHER SIDE IS DESPERATE WHEN THEY BRING UP CENSORSHIP . . .
DR, HENNINGS, HAVE YOU EVER HEARD OF THE FIRST AMENDMENT?
OF COURSE! AND I'M A FIRM BELIEVER IN IT.
BUT FREE SPEECH CAN BE ABUSED. AND IT'S NOT JUST HORROR STORIES THAT PLAGUE OUR YOUNG. PUBLIC LIBRARIES GIVE A CHILD UNLIMITED ACCESS TO OBJECTIONABLE MATERIAL . . .
THE DIARY OF ANNE FRANK IS TOO DISTURBING FOR A CHILD. HUCKLEBERRY FINN IS LACED WITH RACIST LANGUAGE. ALL OF HEMINGWAY'S WORKS ARE SEXIST AT BEST AND MISOGYNISTIC AT WORST.
AND FAIRY TALES-- WELL! THEY'RE EVEN MORE VIOLENT THAN SATURDAY MORNING CARTOONS! WITH ALL THOSE BEHEADINGS AND PEOPLE BEING EATEN-- CHILDREN SHOULDN'T BE EXPOSED TO THAT!
FOR THE SAKE OF THE CHILDREN, I'VE LOBBIED TO HAVE OUR LIBRARIES PULL THOSE BOOKS!
NO FURTHER QUESTIONS, YOUR HONOR . . .
ALANNA WOLFF COULDN'T ARGUE WITH THOSE FACTS. I UNDERSTAND SHE DOESN'T HAVE CHILDREN . . . IF SHE DID, I BET SHE'D SEE OUR POINT A WHOLE LOT BETTER!
WELL, I DON'T HAVE CHILDREN, EITHER- BUT I DO HAVE A DEGREE IN CHILD PSYCHOLOGY THAT PROVES I KNOW WHAT I'M TALKING ABOUT!
LET'S GO BACK IN-- THE JUDGE IS READY TO HAND DOWN HIS DECISION . . .

IN MY CHAMBERS, I EXAMINED THE TRANSCRIPTS AND READ SEVERAL OF THE PLAINTIFF'S HORROR STORIES . . .
THE STORIES SHOW A PREOCCUPATION WITH ROTTED CORPSES RETURNING FROM THE DEAD TO SEEK REVENGE, DECAPITATED HEADS, DISMEMBERED HANDS, AND SO FORTH . . .
THE STORIES TEND TO FOLLOW A FORMULA. I RECALL ONE IN PARTICULAR-- A HUSBAND SUSPECTS HIS WIFE OF BEING A VAMPIRE BUT SHE TURNS OUT TO BE WEREWOLF. EVEN I SAW THAT ONE COMING!
BUT THIS IS THE PLAINTIFF'S STYLE OF STORY-TELLING. SUBTLE AS A BRICK, THE "SNAP ENDINGS" DELIVER POETIC JUSTICE WITH A WINK, A SMILE AND PROBABLY THE PLAINTIFF'S GREATEST OFFENSE: HORRENDOUS PUNS!
OBVIOUSLY, THIS IS NOT TO EVERYONE'S TASTES. THE DE-FENDANTS FIND IT REPREHENSIBLE THAT CHILDREN ARE EXPOSED TO SUCH TALES. WHAT THE DEFENDANTS MUST REALIZE IS THAT STORYTELLERS HAVE BEEN TRYING TO SCARE THE WITS OUT OF CHILDREN FOR CENTURIES-
I REMEMBER READING "THE LEGEND OF SLEEPY HOLLOW" TO MY SON AND WATCHING HIM DEVOUR EVERY WORD AS I DESCRIBED THE HEAD-LESS HORSEMAN . . . JUST LIKE I DID WHEN MY FATHER READ IT TO ME. AND MY GRANDKIDS ARE LOOKING FORWARD TO MY TELLING THEM GHOST STORIES WHEN I TAKE THEM CAMPING NEXT WEEKEND.
IT IS THE COURT'S DECISION THAT IT WOULD BE UNCONSTITUTIONAL TO DENY ACCESS OF THE ALL-HORROR NETWORK TO THOSE PEOPLE IN THIS COUNTY WHO FIND HORROR STORIES HARMLESS.
THOSE WHO ARE OFFENDED BY SUCH STORIES CAN EXERCISE THEIR RIGHT TO CHANGE THE CHANNEL. I FIND FOR THE PLAINTIFF.
COURT IS ADJOURNED
HOW'S THAT FOR POETIC JUSTICE?
YOU MEAN WE WON?
HEY, IT HAPPENS!
I HATE WHEN LAWYERS HIDE BEHIND THE FIRST AMENDMENT! IT JUST CLOUDS THE ISSUE!

AND THE JUDGE MISSED THE POINT! HE SOUNDS AS BAD AS THE BIER-MEISTER IF HE MENTALLY ABUSES HIS GRANDCHILDREN THAT WAY!

JOSETTE?
ARE YOU ALL RIGHT?

MAYBE SHE'S IN SHOCK OVER THE RULING!
JOSETTE! YOU CAN'T BE THAT DISAPPOINTED. WHAT'S GOT INTO-

YOOOOU?!

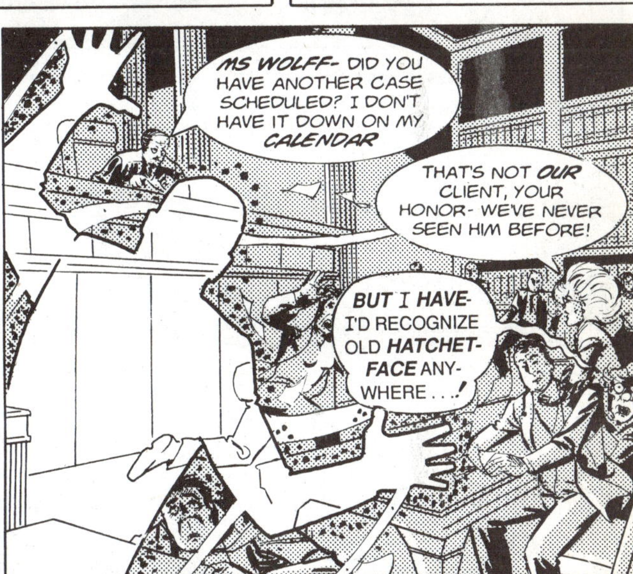
MS WOLFF- DID YOU HAVE ANOTHER CASE SCHEDULED? I DON'T HAVE IT DOWN ON MY CALENDAR
THAT'S NOT OUR CLIENT, YOUR HONOR- WE'VE NEVER SEEN HIM BEFORE!
BUT I HAVE- I'D RECOGNIZE OLD HATCHET-FACE ANY-WHERE...!

IT'S DR. FORREST BERTRUM!!

BERTRUM? HE WASN'T ON THE WITNESS LIST!
BESIDES, HE'S TOO LATE! THE JUDGE ALREADY RULED!
DON'T YOU GUYS KNOW A "SNAP ENDING" WHEN YOU SEE IT? HE'S COMING BACK FOR REVENGE!!

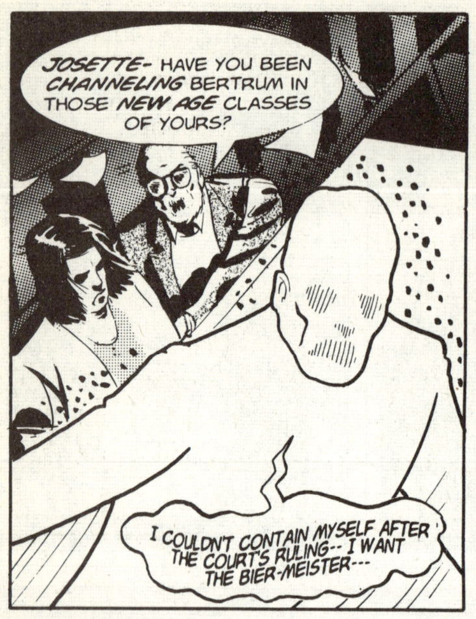
JOSETTE- HAVE YOU BEEN CHANNELING BERTRUM IN THOSE NEW AGE CLASSES OF YOURS?
I COULDN'T CONTAIN MYSELF AFTER THE COURT'S RULING-- I WANT THE BIER-MEISTER---

--- SO I CAN APOLOGIZE!
HE'S A COMIN' FOR ME!! HE'S--
-DID HE SAY APOLOGIZE?!
LET'S HEAR HIM OUT, OKAY?
IT'S A LITTLE LATE FOR APOLOGIES, DON'T YOU THINK, DR. BERTRUM? YOU RUINED MY CLIENT'S CAREER 40 YEARS AGO!

I WAS WRONG!! HOW COULD I HAVE BEEN SO FOOLISH TO THINK SILLY HORROR STORIES COULD TURN CHILDREN INTO CRIMINALS?! CRIME NEVER DROPPED AFTER THE HORROR HOSTS WERE BANNED!!
THE VERY CHILDREN I WANTED TO PROTECT HATED ME ALL THEIR LIVES--

--- THEY CURSED ME NEVER TO REST FOR DEPRIVING THEM OF THEIR ENTERTAINMENT! AND IF THAT WASN'T BAD ENOUGH---

--- DO-GOODERS KEEP EVOKING MY SPIRIT!!
- AND THROUGH THEM, FOR ALL ETERNITY, I'M DAMNED TO RELIVE THE SAME MISTAKE OVER AND OVER-- TRYING TO PROTECT THE CHILDREN...

...THE CHILDREN...

EPILOGUE
BIERIE, LET ME ASK YOU- IS IT POSSIBLE THOSE KIDS LEARNED HOW TO PUT SUCH A CURSE ON BERTRUM FROM ONE OF YOUR STORIES?
COULD BE . . . HEH HEH BUT I'LL NEVER ADMIT THAT OLD QUACK MIGHT'VE HAD A POINT ALL ALONG . . . !
GERSHON-- WHAT HAPPENED . . . THE RULING . . . ?
JOSETTE, REMEMBER THAT FEELING YOU HAD IN YOUR BONES? WELL, GUESS WHAT . . . !
WELL, WITH THE RULING IN YOUR FAVOR, IT LOOKS LIKE YOU'LL BE BACK ON THE AIR . . .
EVEN THOUGH JUDGE DEWEY SAYS HE WON'T LET HIS GRANDKIDS WATCH YOUR SHOW!
AND HOW ABOUT THAT JUDGE? I WAS EXPECTING THE WORST-- I HEARD HIS NICKNAME IS "THE HANGING JUDGE" . . . !
IT IS--

"JUDGE DEWEY LIKES TO HAVE HIS PICTURE TAKEN WITH CELEBRITY LITIGANTS THAT GO BEFORE HIS BENCH-- YOU SHOULD SEE THE PHOTOS HANGING IN HIS CHAMBERS!

YEAH- SOME CELEBRITY! I'M FLAT BROKE UNTIL THE NETWORK COUGHS UP SOME MOOLAH! AND I SHUDDER TO THINK WHAT YOUR LEGAL BILL WILL BE . . . !
GETTING YOU OUT OF JAIL WAS PRO BONO, BIERIE . . . AS FOR REPRESENTING THIS CASE, A FAN OFFERED TO PICK UP THE TAB . . .

AND I'M HONORED TO DO SO! I MUST APOLOGIZE FOR FAILING TO RECOGNIZE YOU IN ALANNA'S OFFICE. WHEN I WAS TOLD WHO YOU WERE, I WAS STUNNED!
YOU WERE AN INSPIRATION TO ME AS A CHILD! IN FACT, YOUR STORIES WERE WHAT MADE ME GO INTO HORROR WRITING. DO FORGIVE ME- I'M FAWNING . . .
NILES PIB?! A FAN OF MINE? FAWN AWAY . . .

I'LL NEVER FORGET- I WAS A LAD OF TEN LISTENING TO YOUR TALE OF A BELEAGURED HUSBAND WHO SUSPECTED THAT HIS WIFE WAS A VAMPIRE . . . NEVER DREAMING SHE WAS REALLY A . . .
HOW MANY TIMES AM I GOING TO HEAR THAT STORY?
OH, BYRD, IT'S A CLASSIC!

OH, YOU SWEET, WONDERFUL MAN! THIS IS JUST THE ICING ON THE CAKE FOR THIS HOSTESS!
HOSTESS? YOU MEAN-- ?

YEP! EVERY INCH A WOMAN, DREAMBOAT!
BUT-- DON'T THEY CALL YOU THE BIER-MEISTER . . . ?
HEY, A PUN'S A PUN, NILES . . .
HEH-HEH THERE'S THE OLD BIER BELLE NOW!

HEH . . . WE KNEW YOU HAD A GOOD CASE!
WE WERE BEHIND YOU 100%!

THIS CALLS FOR A CELEBRATION . . .
YEAH, A TOAST TO THAT OLD HORROR TRADITION!

HUH? THE BIER-MEISTER WALKED RIGHT PAST US!
WHAT'S HER PROBLEM?
WHY IS SHE MAD AT US? WE DIDN'T DO ANYTHING!
ROID RAGE
THE ONLY GAME YOU NEED A MOP TO PLAY.
MEG
. . . SOMETHING INSIDE ME TELLS ME THESE VIDEO GAMES WILL HAVE A LONGLASTING HARMFUL EFFECT ON OUR KIDS! I THINK WE SHOULD ALERT OUR CONGRESSPERSON . . .
I AGREE. I'M NOT FOR CENSORSHIP, BUT . . . !

WOLFF & BYRD COUNSELORS OF THE MACABRE

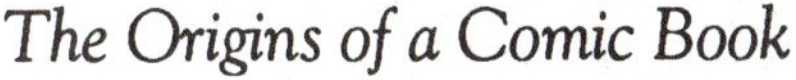

The Origins of a Comic Book

by Batton Lash

Welcome to the Case Files of Wolff & Byrd, Counselors of the Macabre, collecting the first four issues of the W&B comic book. For those of you who are meeting Alanna and Jeff for the first time, let me assure you that our counselors have had a long and checkered career. Okay, maybe *I'm* the one with the checkered career—I've been writing and drawing W&B as a newspaper strip for weekly publication since September 1979. I had pitched the strip idea to *The Brooklyn Paper* that summer (after spending several months drawing ads, caricatures, and editorial cartoons for them), insisting every newspaper should have a comic strip. Publisher Ed Weintrob and then-editor Beverly Cheuvront gave me the go-ahead to develop something. The pay was low (believe me, l-o-w!), but I was able to keep the rights.

At the time, *The Brooklyn Paper* was distributed chiefly along Court Street, which is chock full of courthouses and office buildings bursting with law firms. I discovered that while drawing for the paper paid very little, the real money was in delivering it! So on publication day, I'd go with the rest of the paper's minions and dutifully drop off the latest issue. I noticed that every office I delivered to was made up of attorneys. There seemed to be an abundance of small firms. Old-fashioned glass doors. The smell of paper and old leather reeking in the halls and at the front desks. Wouldn't it be funny if it smelled like fire and brimstone at one firm? The buildings on Court Street are these great old prewar structures. (If you're ever in Brooklyn, check out 44 and 32 Court). I'd walk through atmospheric (almost gothic!) halls, deliver two copies per office, go down a wrought-iron flight of stairs to the next floor, Eisneresque shadows draping the walls, and repeat the process.

It was during this routine, I'd think what a great setting for horror it would be—but the horror of the mundane: seeing the shape of a werewolf howling behind a frosted door as his attorney is giving him bad news, or the victim of a vampire, sitting in a lawyer's office, wearing a neck brace, waiting to go to court. The more papers I delivered, the more ridiculous the

Here's how Alanna and Jeff looked in the very first sketch of the partners.

FREE CONSULTATION
for all Vampires, Werewolves, and Things That Go BUMP In The Night.

Hey! Somebody has to defend them.

WOLFF & BYRD
COUNSELORS of the MACABRE

COMING SOON TO
THE NATIONAL LAW JOURNAL

A promo for the strip's debut in *The National Law Journal*..

ideas got. I was supposed to come up with a comic strip to propose to the paper, but instead I found myself distracted by thinking of what kind of lawsuits monsters might take to a Court Street lawyer. Hey, wait a minute . . . ! Is it possible the strip's right under my nose? Well, DUH!

I worked up some sketches for Bev. I always liked the idea of male-female partners in business. They'd be friends, not lovers. This idea has appealed to me ever since I used to watch "The Avengers." They had repartee and best of all, Steed and Mrs. Peel liked and respected each other as equals! I had the names Wolff & Byrd left over from a previous (unrelated to comics) project and went with it. I based W&B's appearance on the actress Sally Kellerman (a long-time favorite of mine) and playwright Moss Hart (I was reading his autobiography, *Act One*, at the time). At least, that's what they were supposed to look like! As you can see in the strip below, the drawing was a tad raw when W&B made their first appearance (this was actually the second strip; the previous one served as a "teaser"). Luckily, *The Brooklyn Paper* stuck with it as I literally learned on the job.

I should mention that even though I loved comic strips (especially the classic continuity strips like *Terry and the Pirates*, *Dick Tracy*, and *Mary Perkins: On Stage*), my real passion was the comic book medium. I liked the format, which tells a story page after page (as opposed to week after week). What appeals to me about appearing in a newspaper is that people who would *never* buy a comic book will read a comic strip in their paper. So after a year of W&B under my belt, I talked *Brooklyn Paper* publisher Weintrob into letting me add a W&B one-shot, eight-page comic book insert to the weekly. (I was taking my cue from Will Eisner, who created *The Spirit* as a comic book insert for Sunday papers from 1940 to 1952.) The publisher gave in, and I did a brand-new W&B comic book story (their first!) in addition to the weekly strip in late August 1980.

A few things, ahem, hindered the project from ever continuing: (a) Since the publisher thought the comic book insert was a crazy idea, I had to do the story (gulp!) *pro bono*; (b) the extra paper, production, and hand-inserting of the comic into 50,000 papers was expensive and time consuming; and (c) I was perhaps a bit too *inexperienced*. (It took me almost two months to do eight pages—not a good pace for a weekly comic book! I can see Eisner shaking his head now.) None of these factors made the idea of a regular comic insert too practical. And maybe I was putting the cart before the horse: I was still feeling my way around the strip—the art needed polish, the stories needed focus, and since the lead characters were lawyers, legal research was needed as well!

Unfortunately, I'm not a lawyer (I can hear all the non-lawyers out there now—"*Unfortunately?!*" Maybe even a few *lawyers* are saying that as well.) When I started W&B, I didn't even know the difference between civil and criminal cases. I spent all my free time (I was working 9 to 5 at an ad agency during this period—did you think I was able to live on doing a strip for peanuts and a comic insert for free?) going to court—as a spectator. I watched the attorneys, lis-

Off-beat courtroom drama! WOLFF & BYRD by Batton Lash

Alanna Wolff and Jeff Byrd's first appearance, in *The Brooklyn Paper*, October 1979.

The very first W&B comic book, an insert to the September 17, 1980 issue of *The Brooklyn Paper.*

tened to arguments, studied the cases, etc.

I had no idea what was going on.

Luckily, over the years, I met many attorneys who were fans of W&B, and they would graciously take the time to explain it all to me, answering technical questions, looking over my scripts to suggest legal jargon, generally adding *verisimilitude* to Wolff & Byrd's practice. I'm very grateful for all their help. (In recent years, attorney Mitch Berger, who works out of Washington, D.C., has helped me immensely on the legal research for both the strip and the four issues reprinted in this book.)

Giving W&B a more "lawyerly" feel came in handy when I was contacted by Tim Robinson, then editor-in-chief of *The National Law Journal*, a weekly publication for the legal profession. Tim saw the strip in *The Brooklyn Paper* and asked if I'd be interested in running W&B in the *Law Journal*. I jumped at the chance for national exposure and worked up a proposal. W&B began in the NLJ in May 1983 and still appears every week.

Over the years, the strip has appeared off and on in various publications (my most recent "steady" being *Comics Buyer's Guide* since 1991), and the response has always been great. (Remember, with the exception of CBG, my audience was the general public.) But I still had a yearning to do comic *books*. A wonderful aspect of the comic book industry is the opportunity for self-publishing, which gives one the chance to compete with the best of 'em! In 1994, I finally took the plunge to produce a regular W&B comic book. (I first delved into the market in 1992, publishing *Supernatural Law*, a collection of W&B strips.)

I must say that I would not be able to do a W&B comic without the support, talent, and efforts of my wonderful wife, Jackie Estrada. Jackie was never less than encouraging when I brought up the idea of self-publishing, and it is because of her that I finally got my act together. Jackie is co-publisher and editor of W&B (awww, look! She's blushing as she copyedits this!). Our first four issues are collected in this volume, and information on obtaining the regular bimonthly W&B comic book is below.

I've been close to Alanna and Jeff for over 16 years. With the advent of their own comic book, I feel like I'm just getting to know them.